To:

From:

DA CROCKYDILE BOOK O'
Frendsheep

Pearls Before Swine Collections

The Sopratos
Da Brudderhood of Zeeba Zeeba Eata
The Ratvolution Will Not Be Televised
Nighthogs
This Little Piggy Stayed Home
BLTs Taste So Darn Good

Treasuries

The Crass Menagerie
Lions and Tigers and Crocs, Oh My!
Sgt. Piggy's Lonely Hearts Club Comic

DA CROCKYDILE BOOK O' Frendsheep

A *Pearls Before Swine* Gift Book by Stephan Pastis

Andrews McMeel
Publishing, LLC

Kansas City

Pearls Before Swine is distributed internationally by United Feature Syndicate.

 For information, write Andrews McMeel Publishing, LLC, an Andrews McMeel Universal company, 1130 Walnut Street, Kansas City, Missouri 64106.

08 09 10 11 12 WKT 10 9 8 7 6 5 4 3 2

ISBN-13: 978-0-7407-7627-4
ISBN-10: 0-7407-7627-4

Library of Congress Control Number: 2008921088

www.andrewsmcmeel.com

Pearls Before Swine can be viewed on the Internet at
www.comics.com

Introduction

We no reely have time to do dis.

Someone juss says, "You guys sooo populars. Do geeft book." And we is like, "Okay. Whatevers. Just pays us monees."

Den dey is say, "Make book about frendsheep." And we is like, "But we ees hate evrybodies." ANd dey is go, "But dat make most monees." So we is like, "Okay. We expert."

So dis is book. Ees about frendsheep.

Peese pay you monees.

The Crocodiles
September 2008

DOES LIVING NEXT DOOR TO A FRATERNITY OF PREDATORS EVER GET TO YOU?
CHUG! CHUG! CHUG!

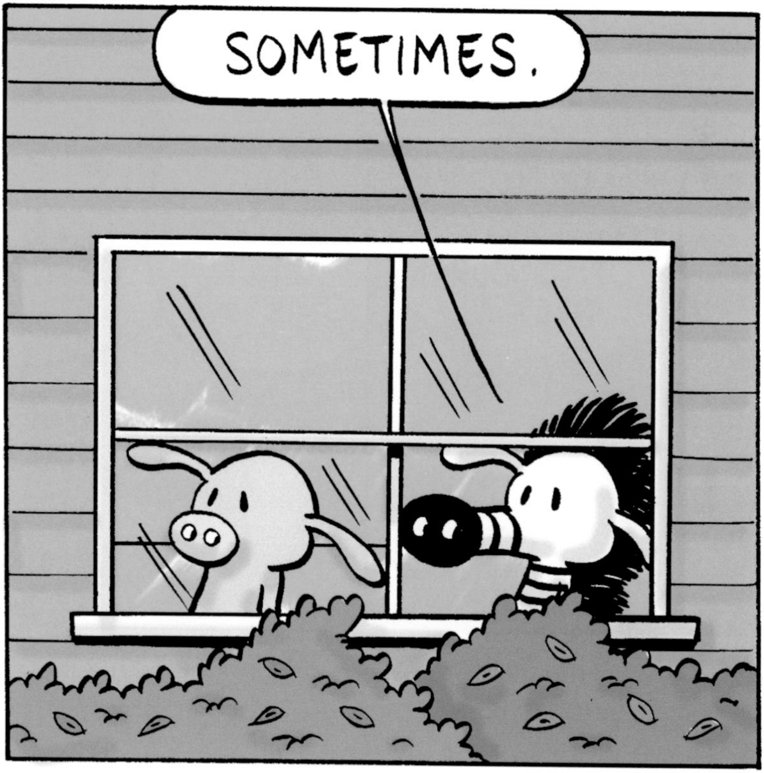
SOMETIMES.

Frends eet ded tings togedder

Hulloooooo, leetle rat... How is you?
WHY DO YOU HAVE A PAIR OF BAGGY JEANS PULLED UP TO YOUR NECK?
Baggy jeans cool. Me a rebel. Girls love.
DUDE, YOU LOOK RIDICULOUS...GUYS WEAR THEIR JEANS REAL LOW NOW.

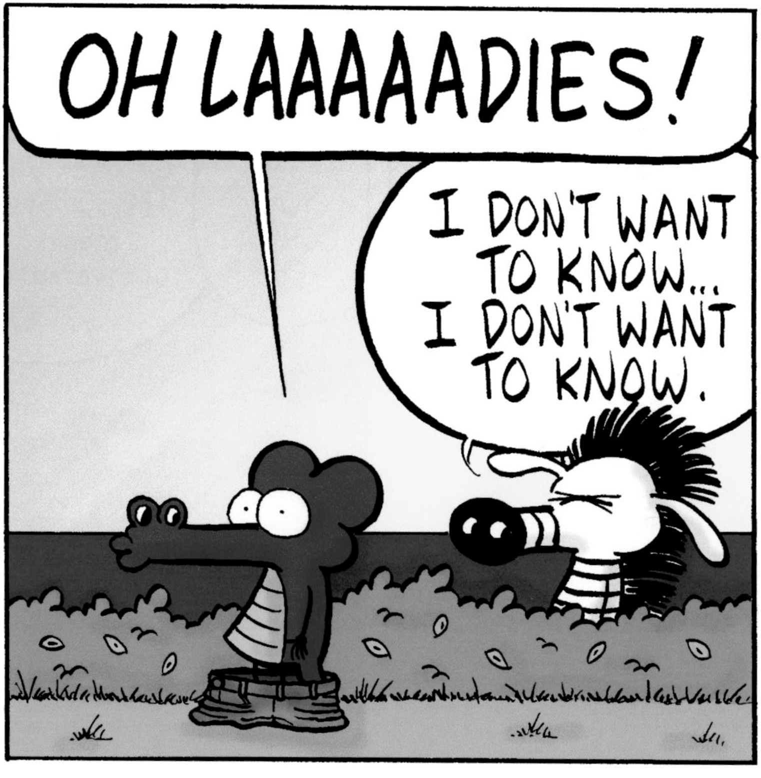
OH LAAAAADIES!
I DON'T WANT TO KNOW... I DON'T WANT TO KNOW.

Frend help yous peek up woomuns

HEY, WHAT'S THE MATTER WITH YOUR FRIEND?
Oh, heem? He choking.
ACK!
AREN'T YOU GONNA HELP?
Oh, no... Death of fellow predator mean less competeetion for prey.
THUD

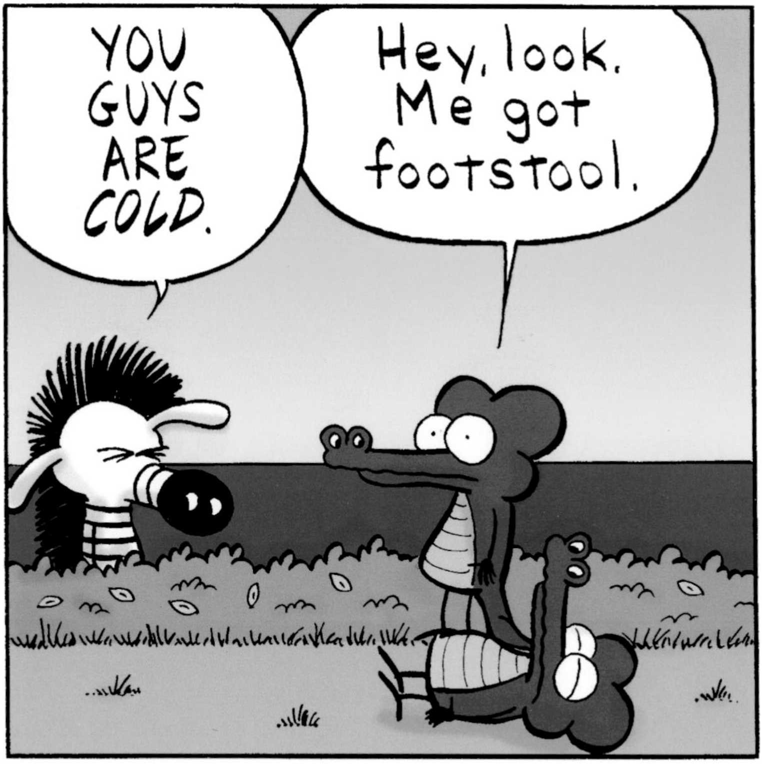
YOU GUYS ARE COLD.
Hey, look. Me got footstool.

Frends suports eech udders.

Okay, zeeba neighba, leesten me. Crocs get costume deepartment. Now we look inteemidating! See, me is Skullhead Doom Guy!!

And me is ballerina!

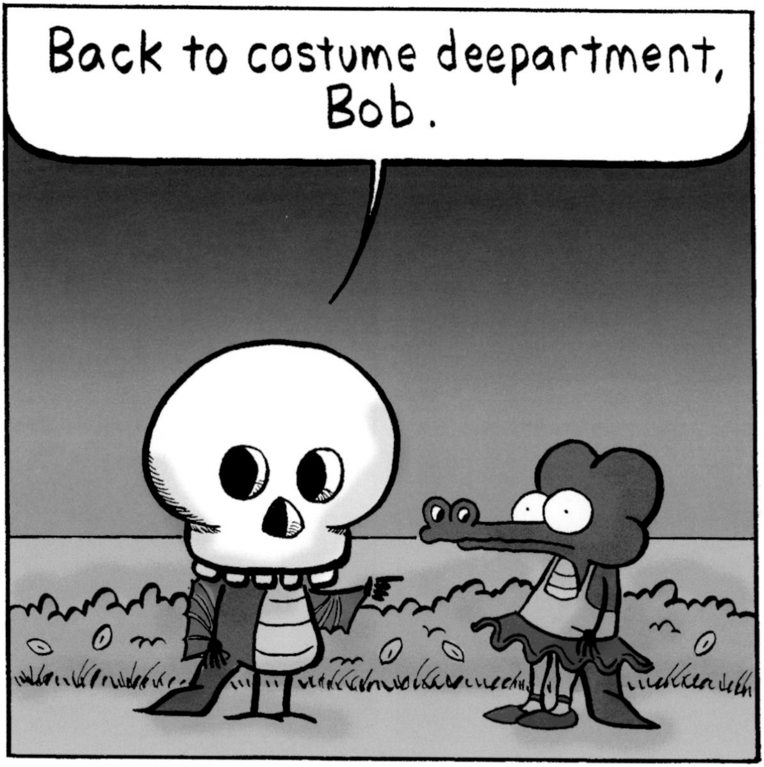
Back to costume deepartment, Bob.

Frends no let frends look wimpee like gurl

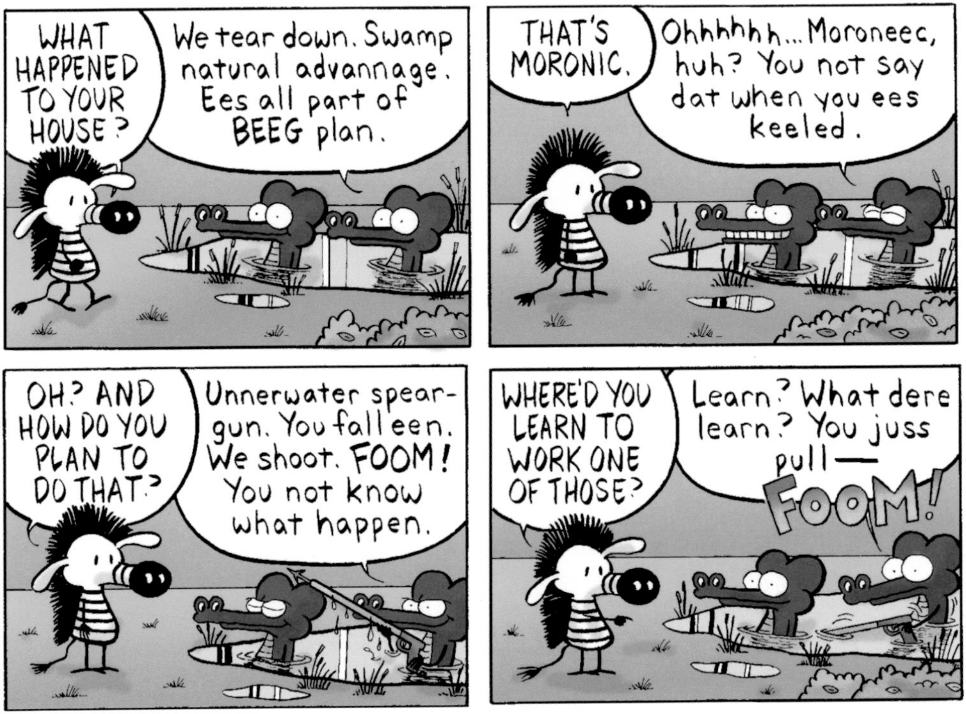
WHAT HAPPENED TO YOUR HOUSE?
We tear down. Swamp natural advannage. Ees all part of BEEG plan.
THAT'S MORONIC.
Ohhhhhh... Moroneec, huh? You not say dat when you ees keeled.
OH? AND HOW DO YOU PLAN TO DO THAT?
Unnerwater spear-gun. You fall een. We shoot. FOOM! You not know what happen.
WHERE'D YOU LEARN TO WORK ONE OF THOSE?
Learn? What dere learn? You juss pull—
FOOM!

Good ting he not know what happen.

Frends sumtime shoots you

JOE'S HANDYMAN SERVICE... JOE SPEAKING.
YEAH...HI...I HAVE A DOGGY DOOR IN MY BACKDOOR THAT THE PREVIOUS OWNER HAD INSTALLED AND I'D LIKE TO GET RID OF IT.
WELL...GENERALLY, THAT MEANS YOU'RE LOOKING AT A WHOLE NEW DOOR, AND THAT CAN RUN YOU ANY-WHERE FROM SIX TO EIGHT HUNDRED BUCKS.
IT'S WORTH EVERY PENNY.

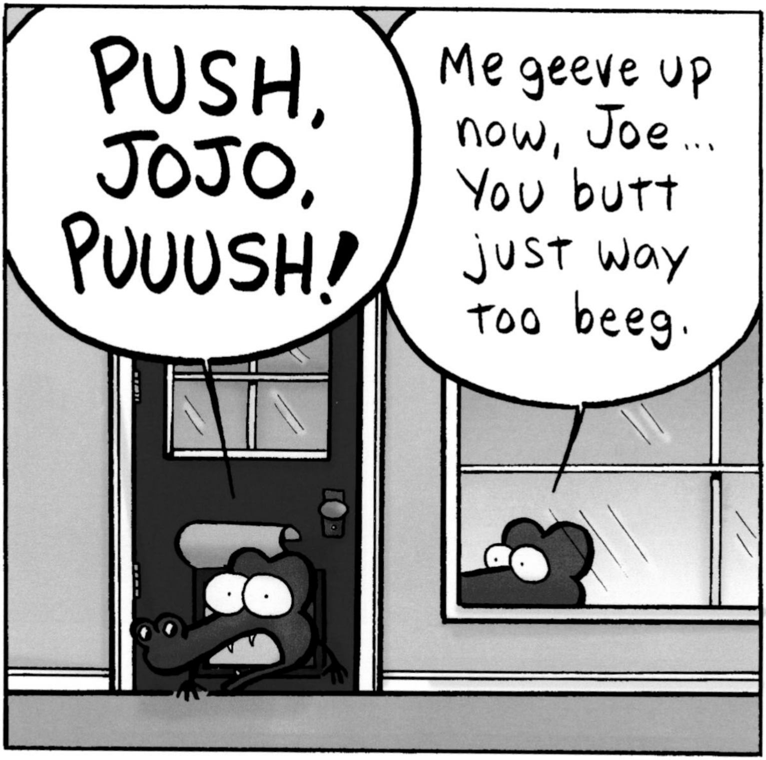
PUSH, JOJO, PUUUSH!
Me geeve up now, Joe... You butt just way too beeg.

If you is have beeg butt, frend sometime honesst and say, "you have beeg butt."

WHAT ARE YOU GUYS DOING?
We bury mines. If you walk in yard, you essplode.
DO *YOU* KNOW WHERE THEY'RE BURIED?
Ah. Gud idea. Larry, go in house. Make map.

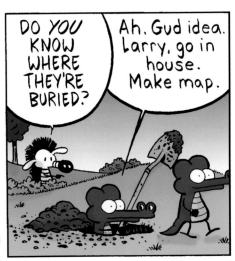

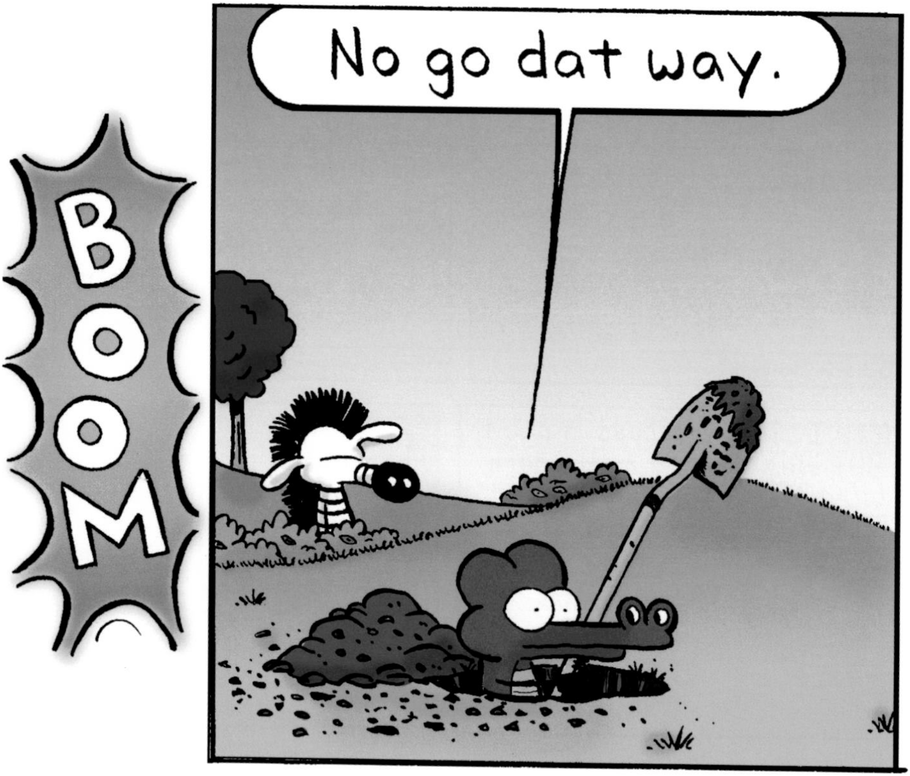
BOOM
No go dat way.

Frends sometimes essplode

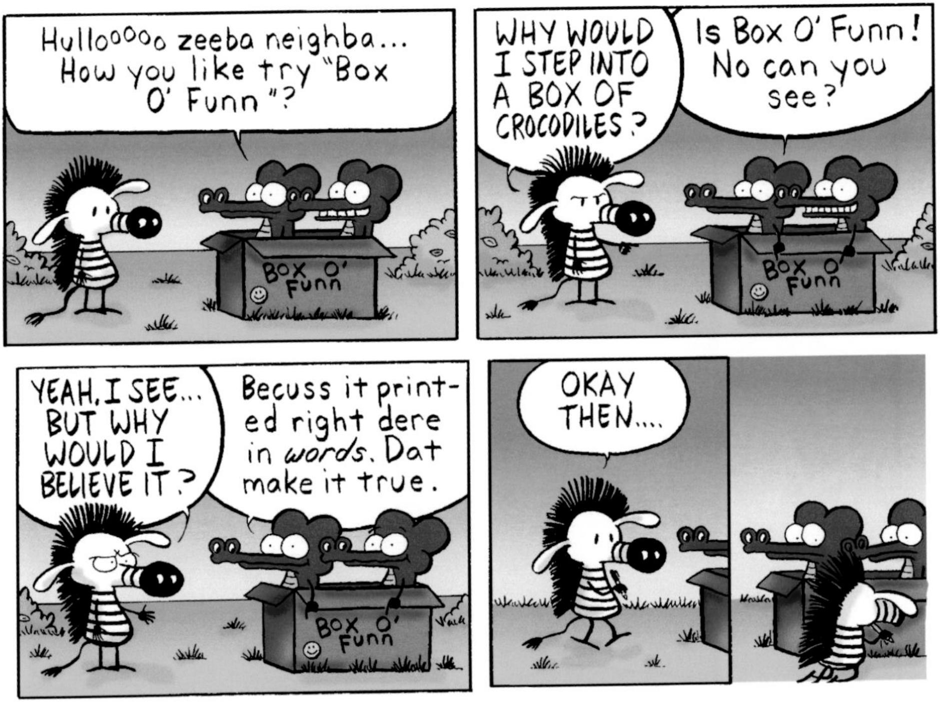
Hulloooo zeeba neighba... How you like try "Box O' Funn"?
BOX O' FUNN
WHY WOULD I STEP INTO A BOX OF CROCODILES?
Is Box O' Funn! No can you see?
BOX O' FUNN
YEAH, I SEE... BUT WHY WOULD I BELIEVE IT?
Becuss it printed right dere in *words*. Dat make it true.
BOX O' FUNN
OKAY THEN....

BOX O' [redacted] Morons
Me want get out now.

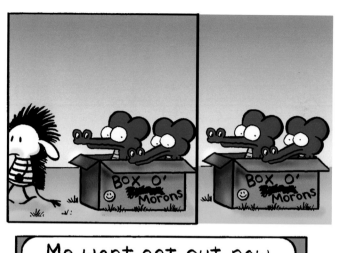

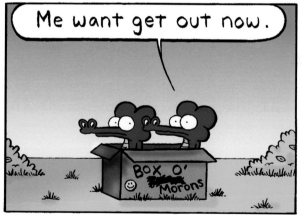

Frends no like beeing called moron by sumone who is even bigger moron like all zeebas

THE CROCODILES SAY THEY BOUGHT A JACUZZI.
A JACUZZI?..... THOSE CROCS ARE BROKE.
THEY SAY THEY FOUND ONE FOR THREE HUNDRED BUCKS.
WHAT KIND OF JACUZZI CAN YOU GET FOR THREE HUNDRED BUCKS?

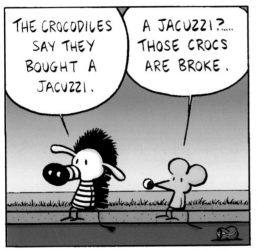

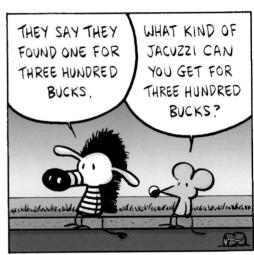

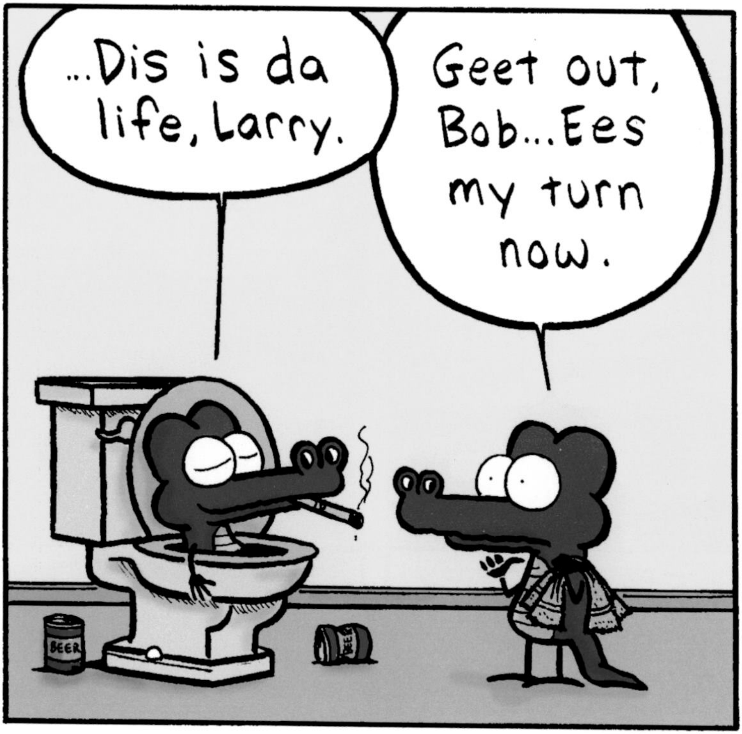
...Dis is da life, Larry.
Geet out, Bob...Ees my turn now.
BEER
BEER

Frends fill house wid cool tings like mebbe you see on MTV Creebs

Pssssst... WANT TO BUY SOME ZEBRA SEEDS? FIFTY BUCKS A BAG.
Haha...We no need seeds. We hunt. We keel. We bad muthas.
Haha. Yeah. What you theenk? Me and Bob desperate losers??
Hahahaha
Heh heh heh.

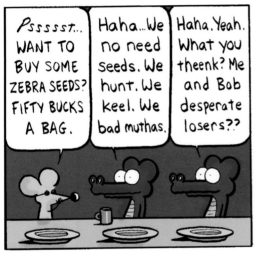

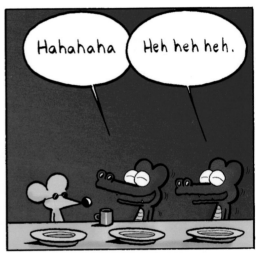

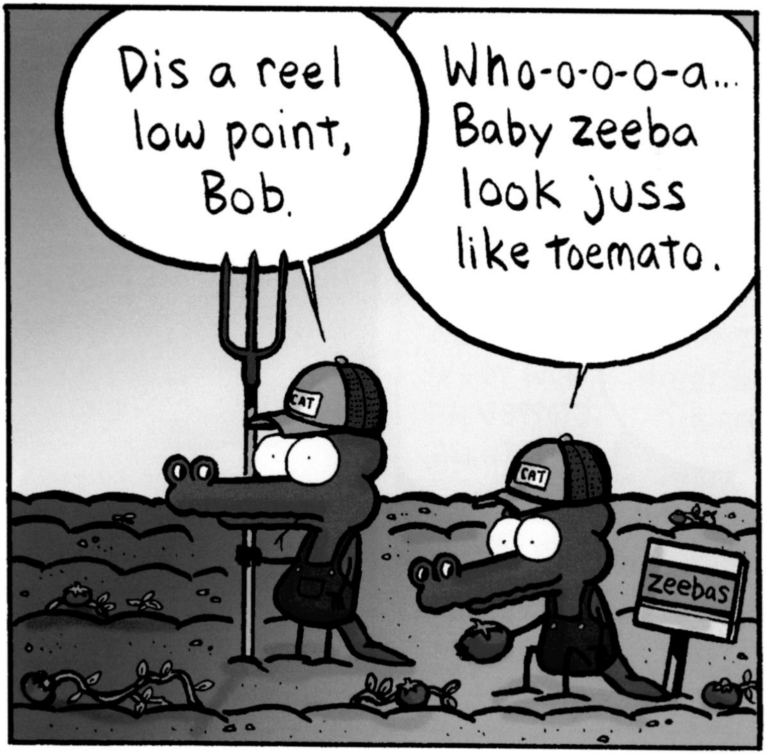
Dis a reel low point, Bob.
Who-o-o-o-a... Baby zeeba look juss like toemato.
CAT
CAT
zeebas

Me not like dis strip. Make crocs look stoopid. No shood be in book

Okay, evil Meester Rat...You sell us zeeba seed, but when we plant, we get toemayto. What you think, we stoopid?
ALL ZEBRAS BEGIN LIFE AS A TOMATO, UNLESS YOU PICK THEM... NOW YOU'VE STOPPED HIS BREATHING.

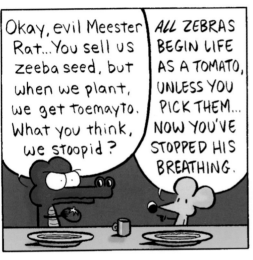

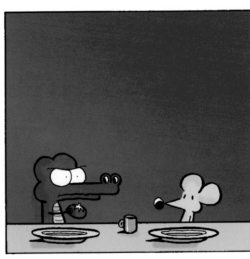

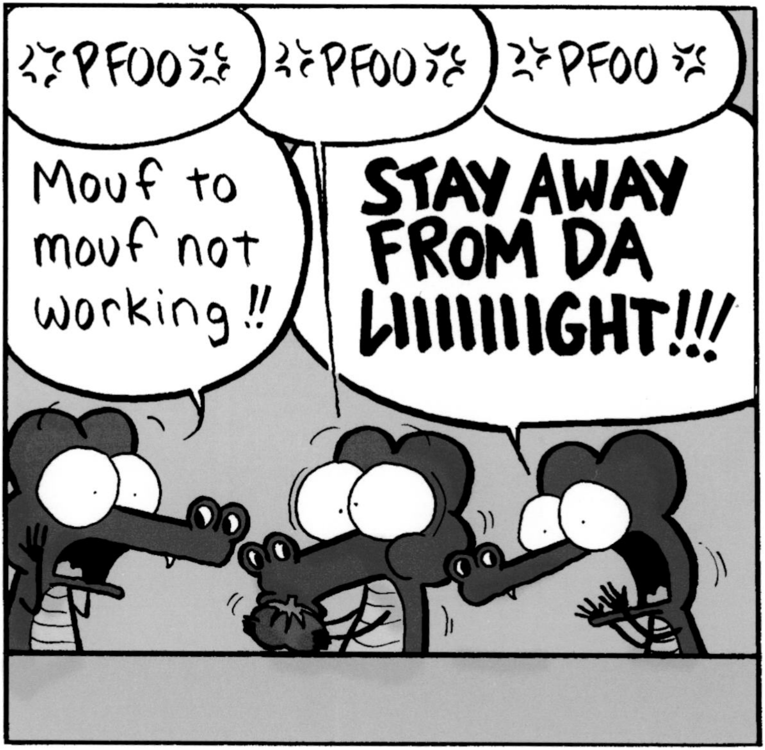
PFOO
PFOO
PFOO
Mouf to mouf not working!!
STAY AWAY FROM DA LIIIIIIIGHT!!!

Dis one worse. Edeetor: No put een bbok

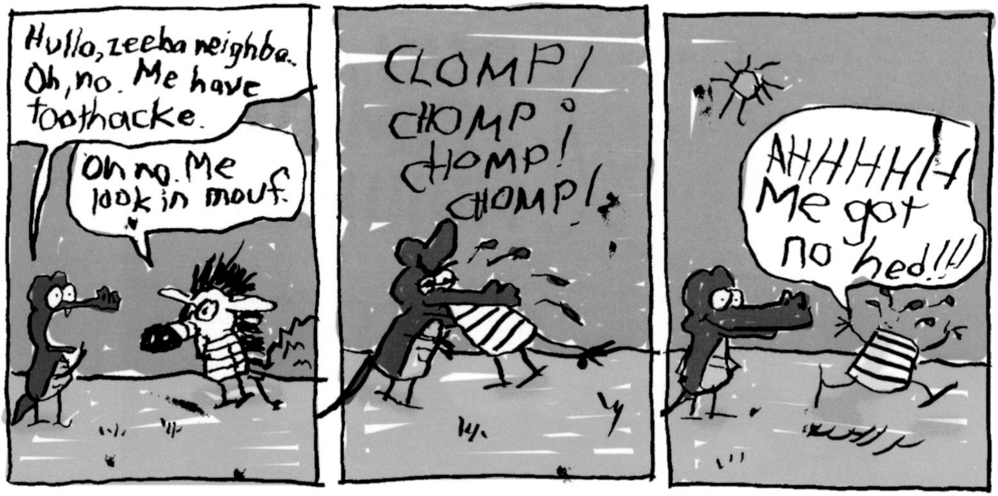
Hullo, zeeba neighba.. Oh, no. Me have toothacke.
Oh no. Me look in mouf.
CLOMP! CHOMP! CHOMP! CHOMP!
AHHHHH! Me got no hed!!!

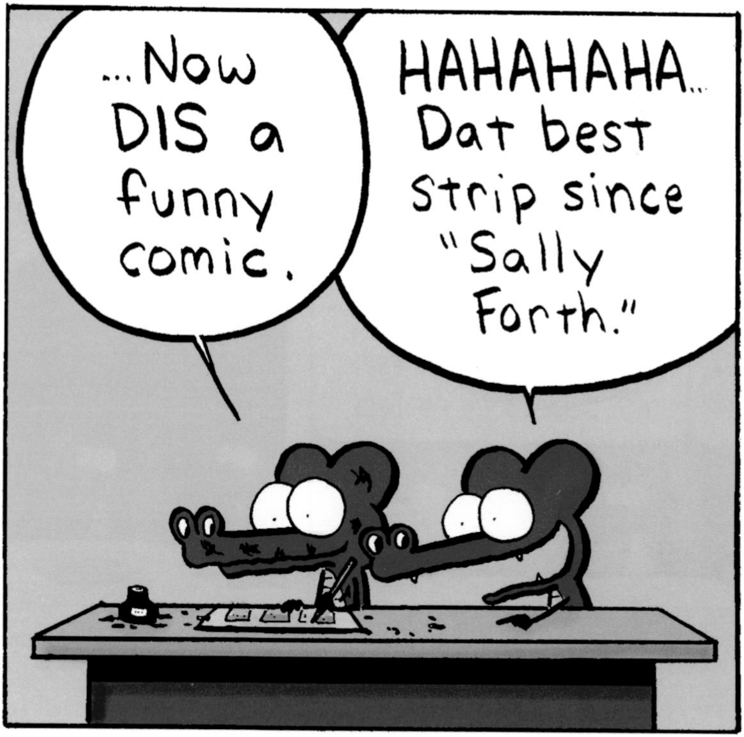
...Now DIS a funny comic.
HAHAHAHA... Dat best strip since "Sally Forth."

Frends know gud humors
when dey is hear it.

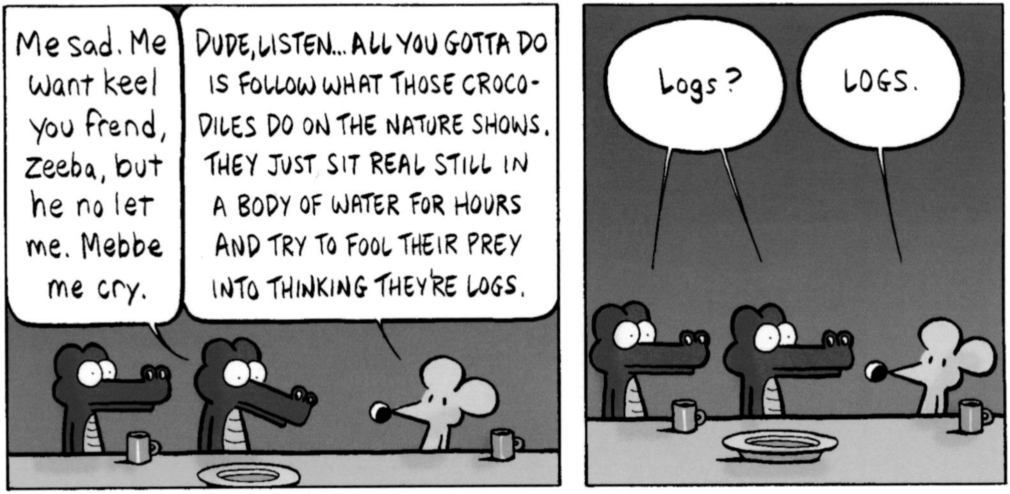
Me sad. Me want keel you frend, zeeba, but he no let me. Mebbe me cry.
DUDE, LISTEN... ALL YOU GOTTA DO IS FOLLOW WHAT THOSE CROCODILES DO ON THE NATURE SHOWS. THEY JUST SIT REAL STILL IN A BODY OF WATER FOR HOURS AND TRY TO FOOL THEIR PREY INTO THINKING THEY'RE LOGS.
Logs?
LOGS.

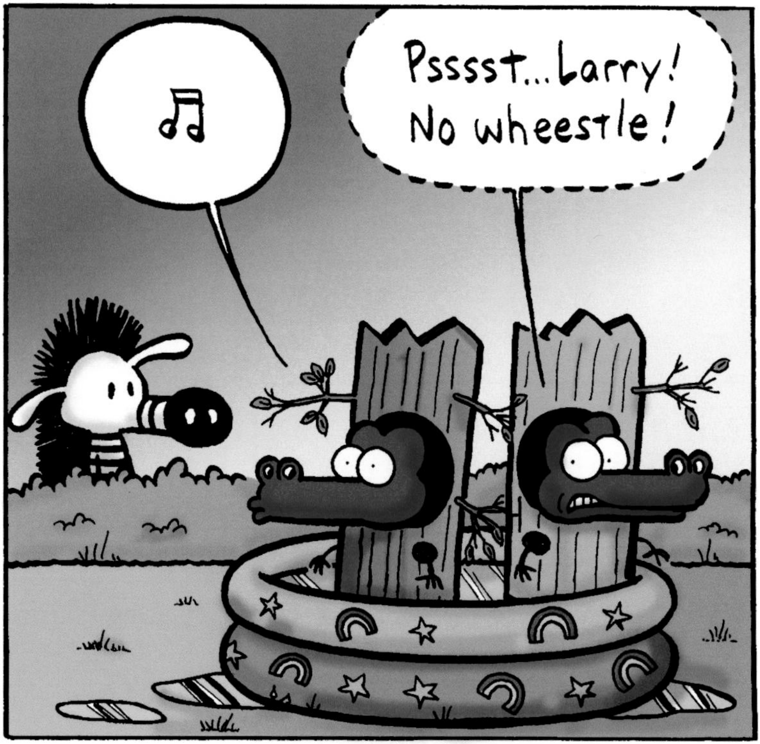
♫
Psssst...Larry!
No wheestle!

Frends no screw tings up like eediot-face larry. me hate him

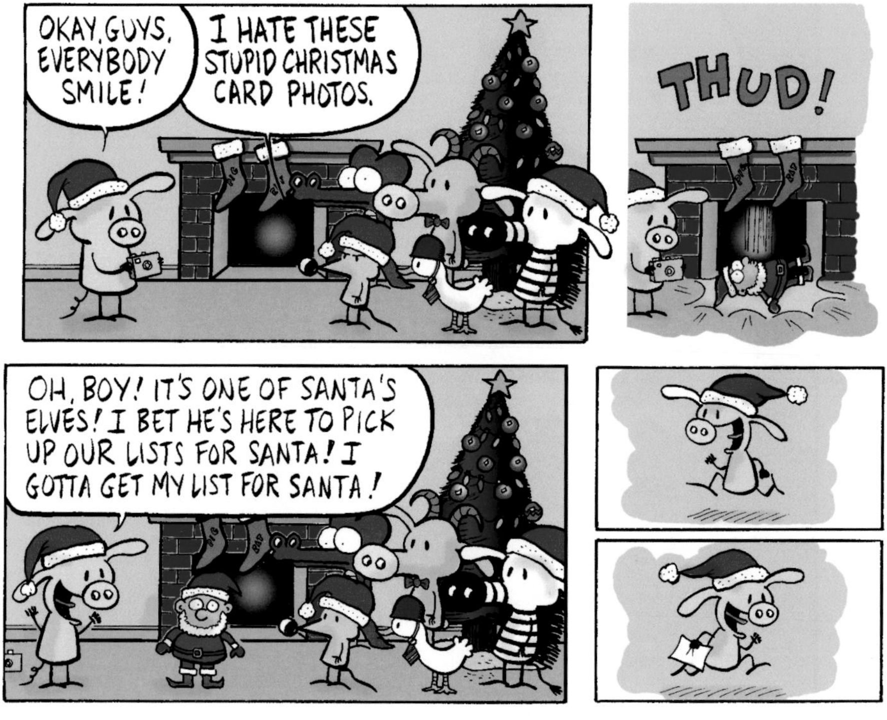
OKAY, GUYS, EVERYBODY SMILE!
I HATE THESE STUPID CHRISTMAS CARD PHOTOS.
THUD!
OH, BOY! IT'S ONE OF SANTA'S ELVES! I BET HE'S HERE TO PICK UP OUR LISTS FOR SANTA! I GOTTA GET MY LIST FOR SANTA!

UURRRRP
OH, THAT IS SOOO NOT IN THE SPIRIT OF CHRISTMAS.

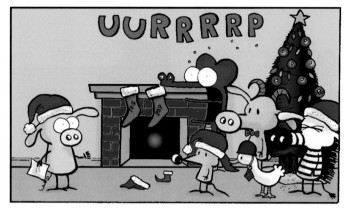

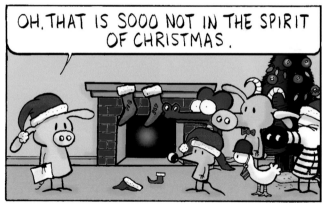

elves is taste like gud chicken. (not reely have to do wid "frendsheep" theme)

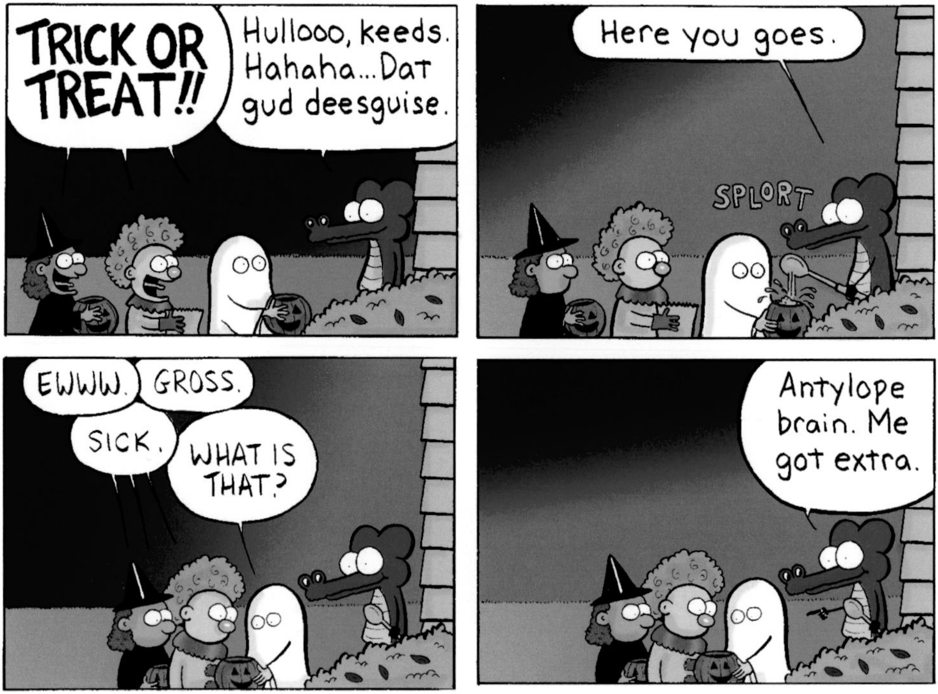
TRICK OR TREAT!!
Hullooo, keeds. Hahaha... Dat gud deesguise.
Here you goes.
SPLORT
EWWW.
GROSS.
SICK.
WHAT IS THAT?
Antylope brain. Me got extra.

AAAAHHHHHH
Spoiled keeds.
Nexx year we turn off porchlight.

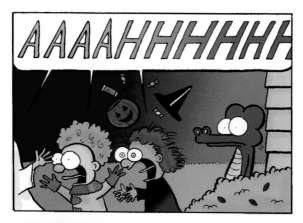

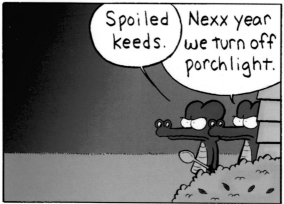

frends mebbe share antylope (but NEVER share elves, becuss elves is taste like gud chicken).

HELLOOOO, CROCODILE NEIGHBOR...LISTEN...
SINCE YOU'VE SPENT A LIFETIME TRYING TO
EAT US, A FEW OF US THOUGHT IT'D BE A
GOOD TIME TO TRY EATING **YOU**....HOW
DOES *THAT* FEEL?

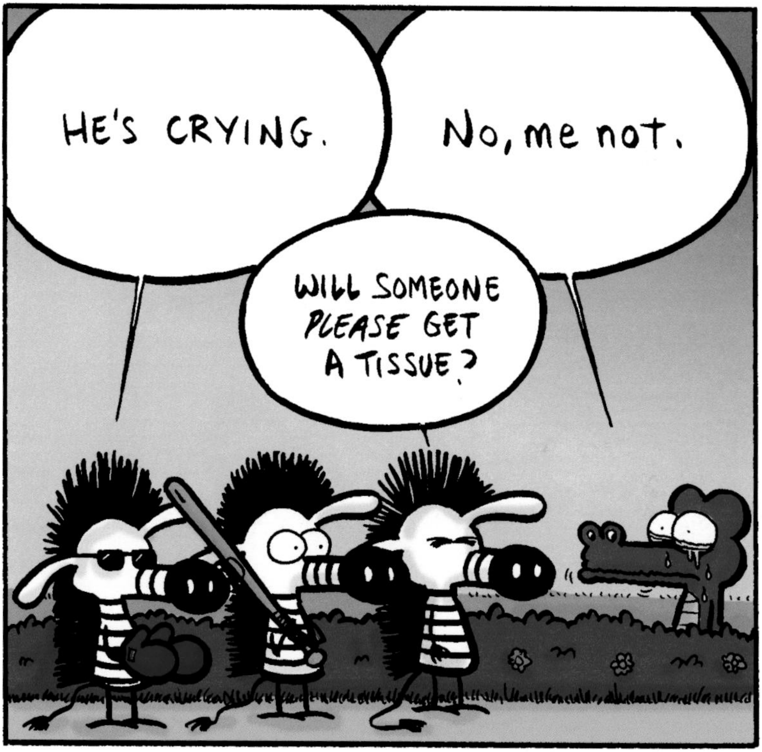
HE'S CRYING.
No, me not.
WILL SOMEONE PLEASE GET A TISSUE?

if you is cry, you no deeserve frend.
becuss you is pansy.

HI... I GOT A SPECIAL DELIVERY.
FLOWERS? WOW, NO ONE EVER SENDS ME FLOWERS!... THAT'S GREAT!... LET ME SEE THE CARD.
Jo's Flowers
Peese die.
1-800-555-5555

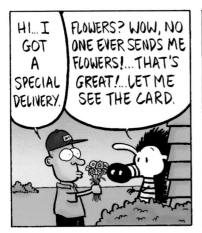

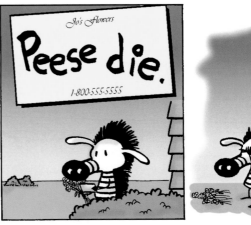

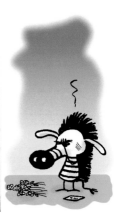

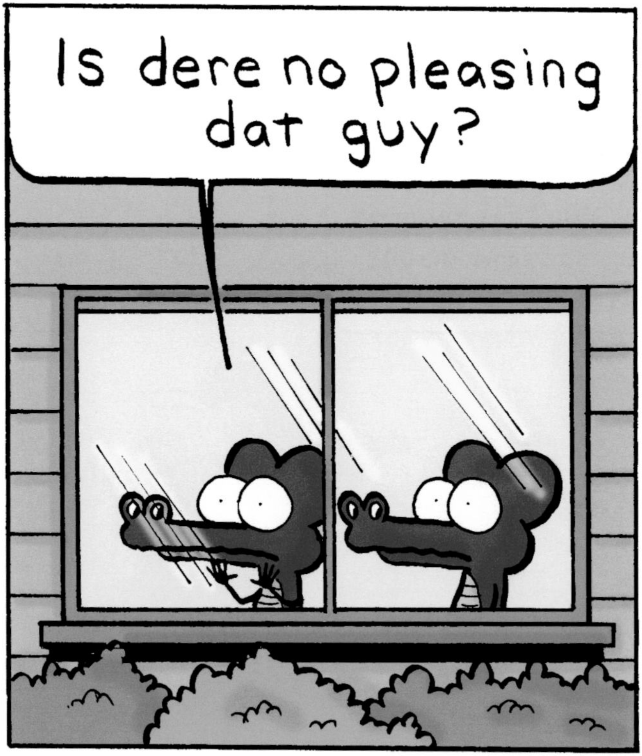
Is dere no pleasing dat guy?

HAHAHAHA me juss like dis becuss zeeba is like, "WHUH?"

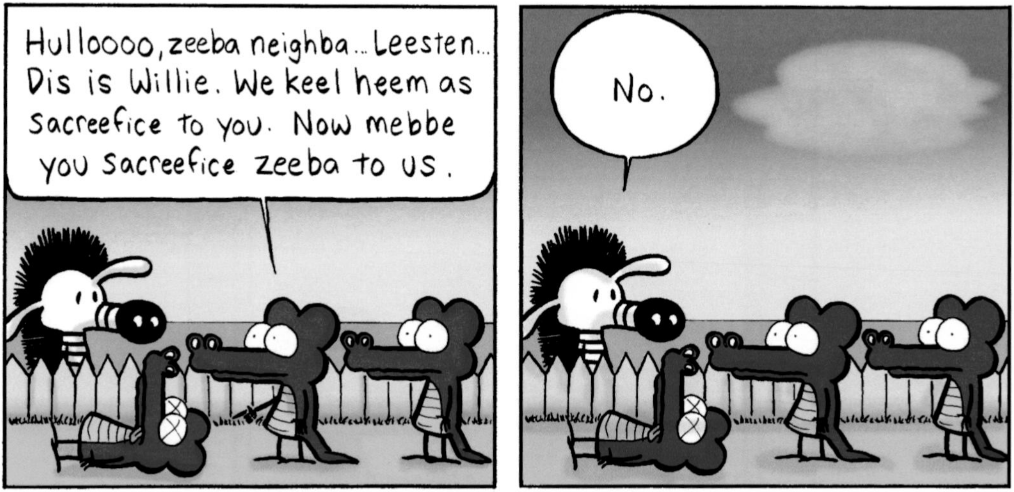
Hulloooo, zeeba neighba... Leesten... Dis is Willie. We keel heem as sacreefice to you. Now mebbe you sacreefice zeeba to us.
No.

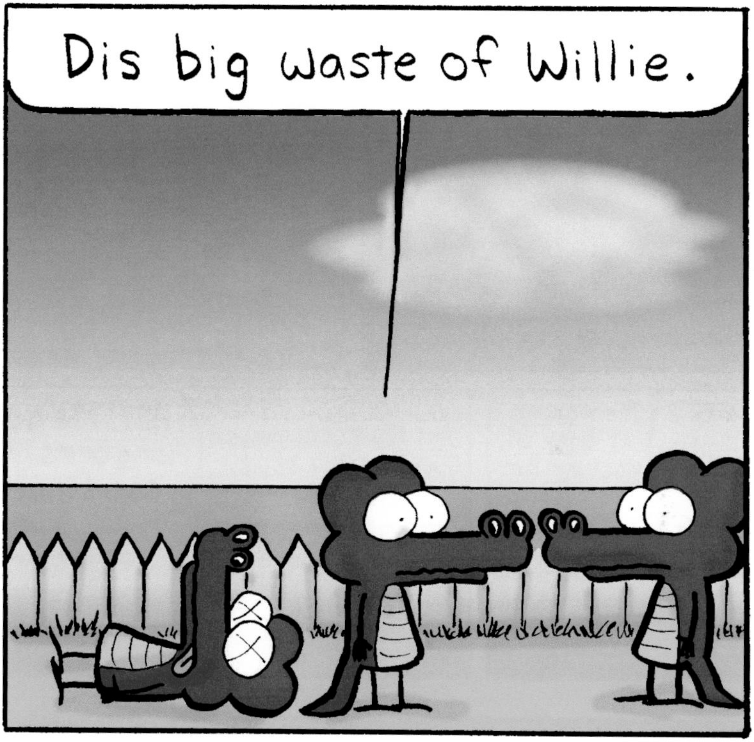
Dis big waste of Willie.

Frends sumtimes take one for teem.

Hulloooooo, zeeba neighba... Leesten... Me need leetle help.
WHY DO YOU HAVE A WOOD CHIPPER ON YOUR FRONT LAWN?
Ohh, dat? Me just doing leetle yard work. But leesten, me tink me lose contakk lens.
WHERE'D YOU LOSE IT?
Me tink it at back of machine. But me no can reach.
GOSH, YOU KNOW.. MY ARMS JUST AREN'T LONG ENOUGH.. GUESS I WON'T BE ABLE TO FIND ——
HEY! Me got long arms! Me can find!!

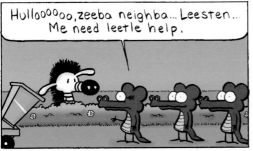

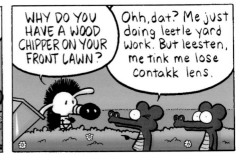

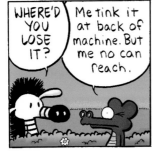

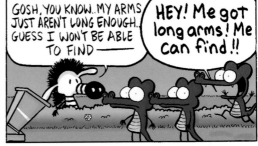

BZZZZZT
Does you find it?!

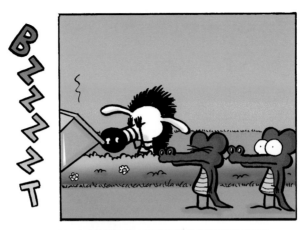

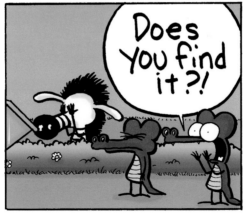

Frends go to MEETENGS before we does assasynations and LEESTENS to PLANN so he no screw tings up by JUMPEENG EEN WOOD CCHEEPER

Okay, zeeba neighba... Put hands in sky. Mebbe we crockydiles no fast enough to catch you, but now we got gun, so you days is numbahed.

BOOM

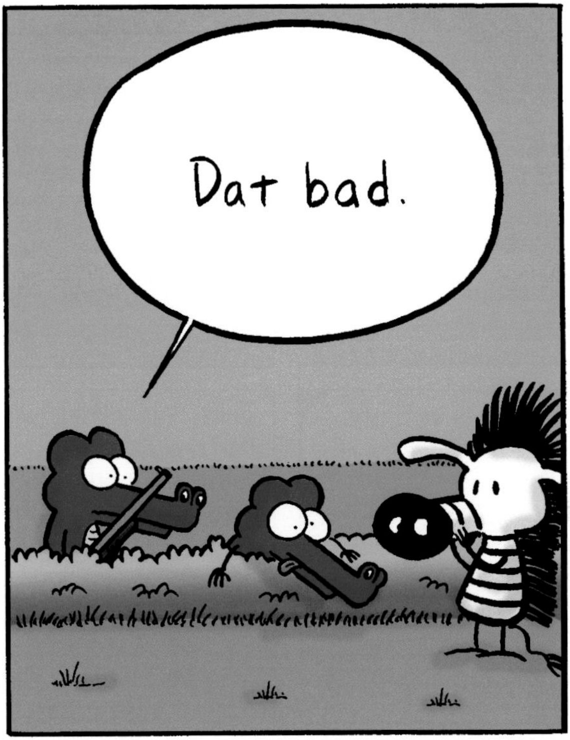
Dat bad.

Frend sumtime make honest meestake

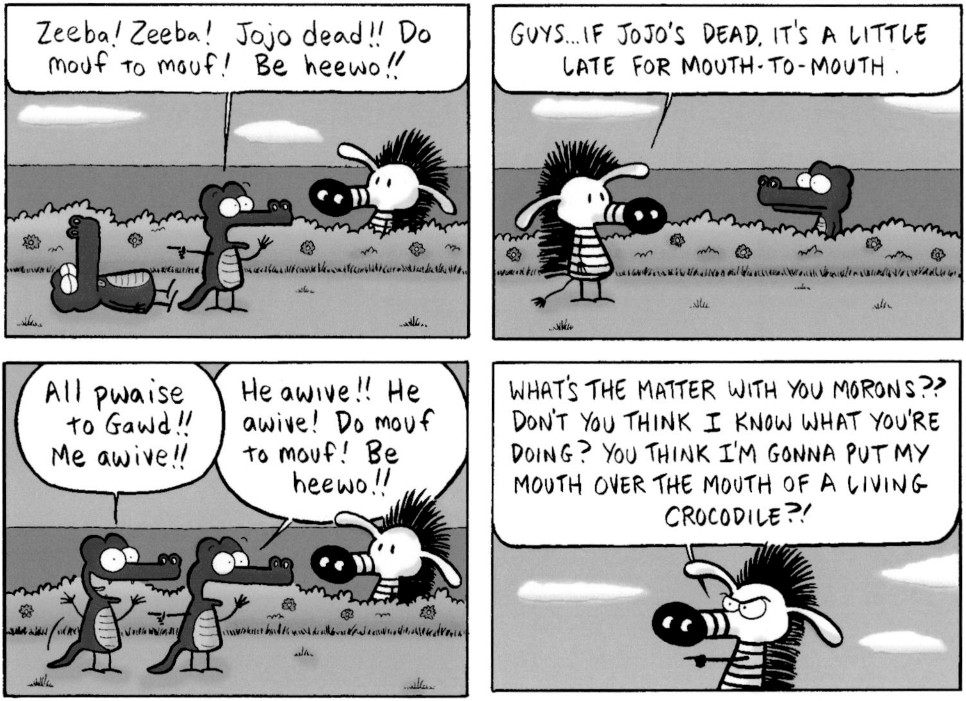
Zeeba! Zeeba! Jojo dead!! Do mouf to mouf! Be heewo!!
GUYS...IF JOJO'S DEAD, IT'S A LITTLE LATE FOR MOUTH-TO-MOUTH.
All pwaise to Gawd!! Me awive!!
He awive!! He awive! Do mouf to mouf! Be heewo!!
WHAT'S THE MATTER WITH YOU MORONS?? DON'T YOU THINK I KNOW WHAT YOU'RE DOING? YOU THINK I'M GONNA PUT MY MOUTH OVER THE MOUTH OF A LIVING CROCODILE?!

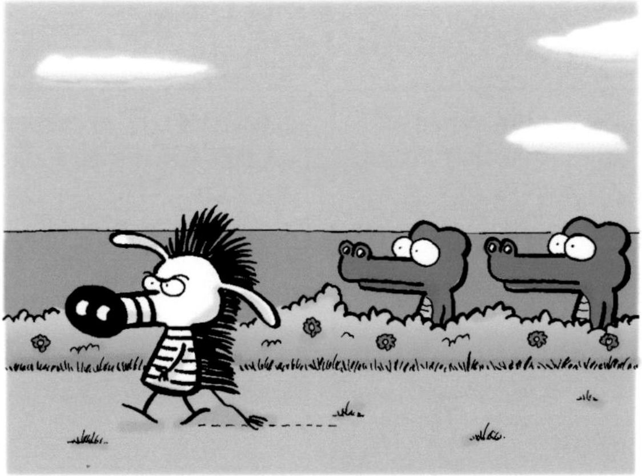

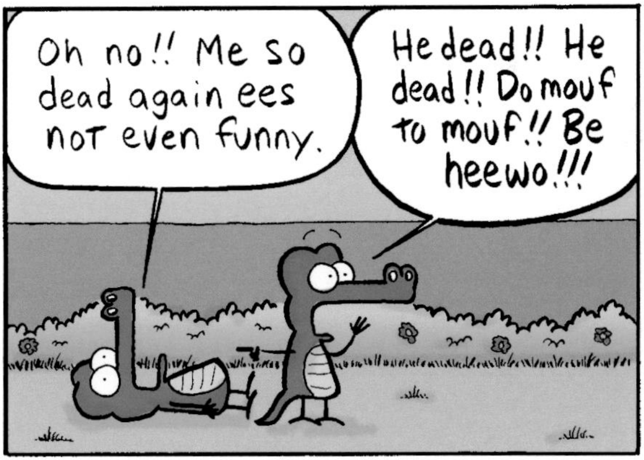
Oh no!! Me so dead again ees not even funny.
He dead!! He dead!! Do mouf to mouf!! Be heewo!!!

[Beeg deel. So dis not work. Why you put in book?]

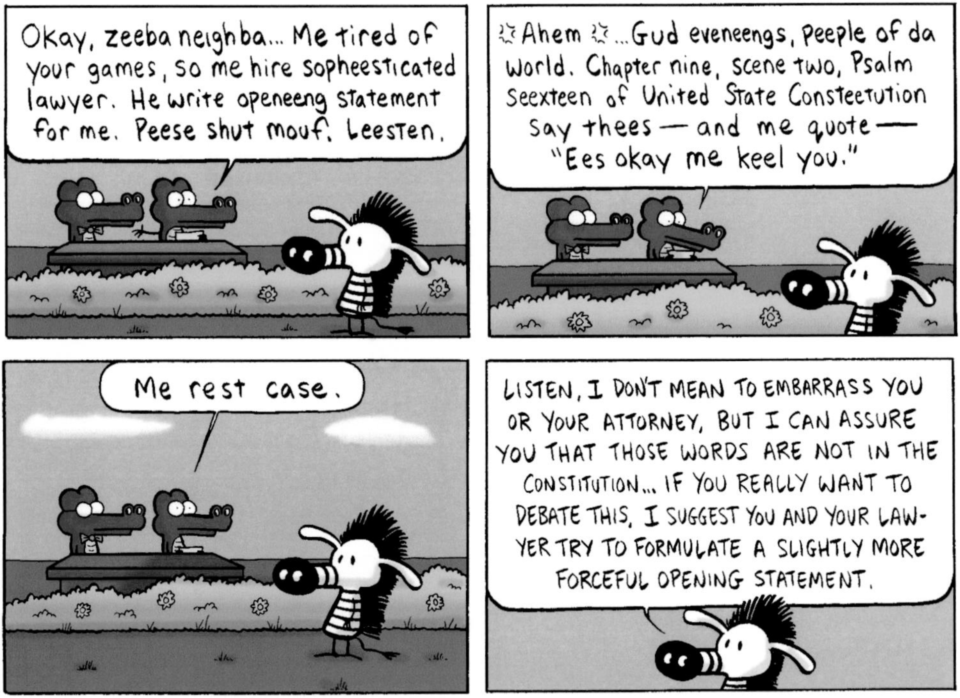
Okay, zeeba neighba... Me tired of your games, so me hire sopheesticated lawyer. He write openeeng statement for me. Peese shut mouf. Leesten.
Ahem ...Gud eveneengs, peeple of da world. Chapter nine, scene two, Psalm seexteen of United State Consteetution say thees — and me quote — "Ees okay me keel you."
Me rest case.
LISTEN, I DON'T MEAN TO EMBARRASS YOU OR YOUR ATTORNEY, BUT I CAN ASSURE YOU THAT THOSE WORDS ARE NOT IN THE CONSTITUTION... IF YOU REALLY WANT TO DEBATE THIS, I SUGGEST YOU AND YOUR LAWYER TRY TO FORMULATE A SLIGHTLY MORE FORCEFUL OPENING STATEMENT.

WHISPER
WHISPER
WHISPER
Your mama fat as house.

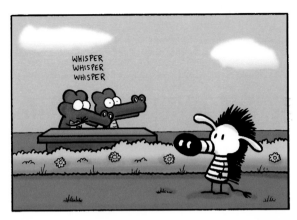

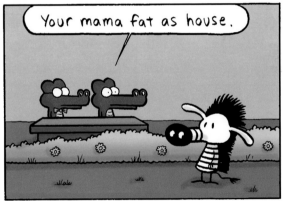

EEN YOU FACESe ZEEBA! HAHAHA

WHAT'S WRONG WITH YOUR FRIEND?
Oh, he have bad heart. Probbly heart attack.
Ack.
AREN'T YOU GONNA HELP?
Why he need help to have heart attack?

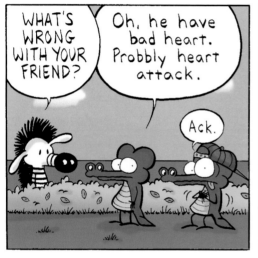

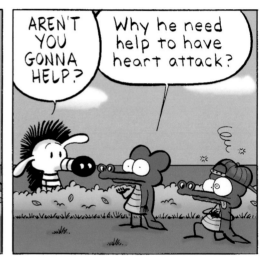

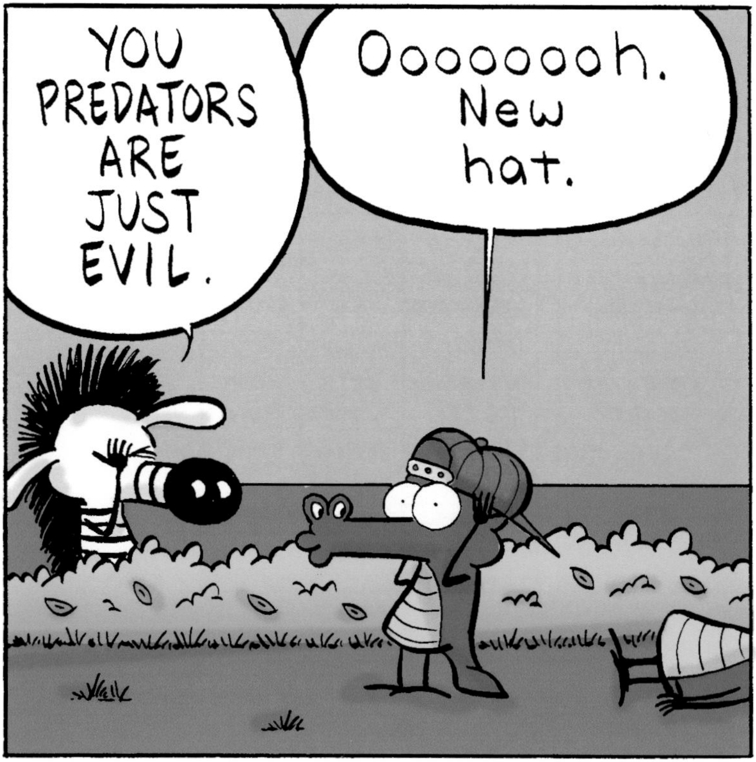
YOU PREDATORS ARE JUST EVIL.
Ooooooooh. New hat.

Frends is share

HI, CAN I HELP— CROCODILES!! WHAT THE.??

No No No No No bad. Good. We new next door neighbor. We start fraternity. See sweater?

A FRATERNITY FOR CROCODILES?! I'VE NEVER HEARD OF SUCH A THING...WHAT'S THE Z.Z.E. STAND FOR?

Oh, dar? Is Greek letters. It mean "Zeta Zeta Epsilon."

But Brudder Joe...You say it mean "Zeba Zeba Eata."

SLAP!!

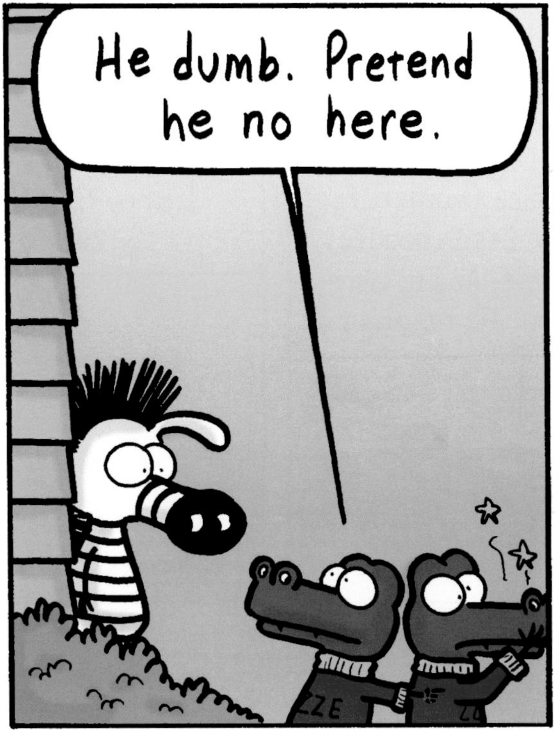
He dumb. Pretend he no here.

Frends slap frends een face if neceesary

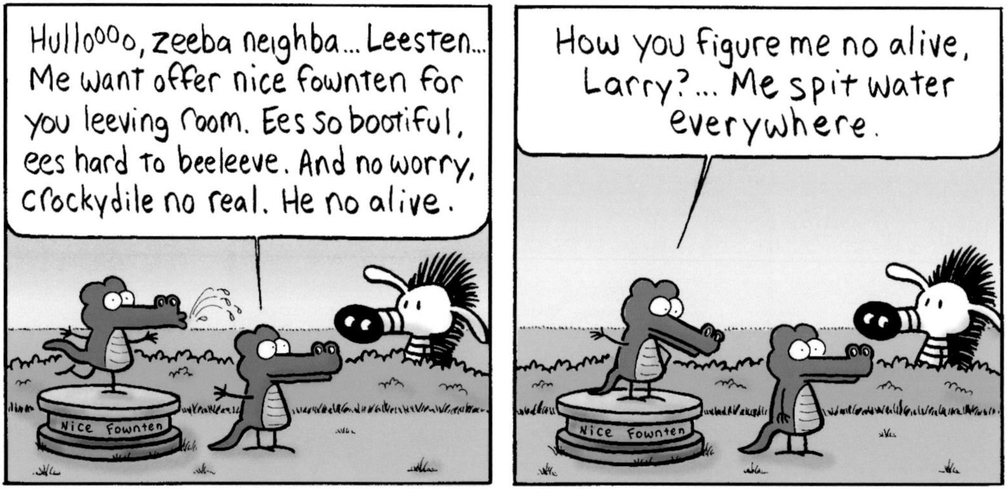
Hulloooo, zeeba neighba... Leesten... Me want offer nice fownten for you leeving room. Ees so bootiful, ees hard to beeleeve. And no worry, crockydile no real. He no alive.
Nice Fownten
How you figure me no alive, Larry?... Me spit water everywhere.
Nice Fownten

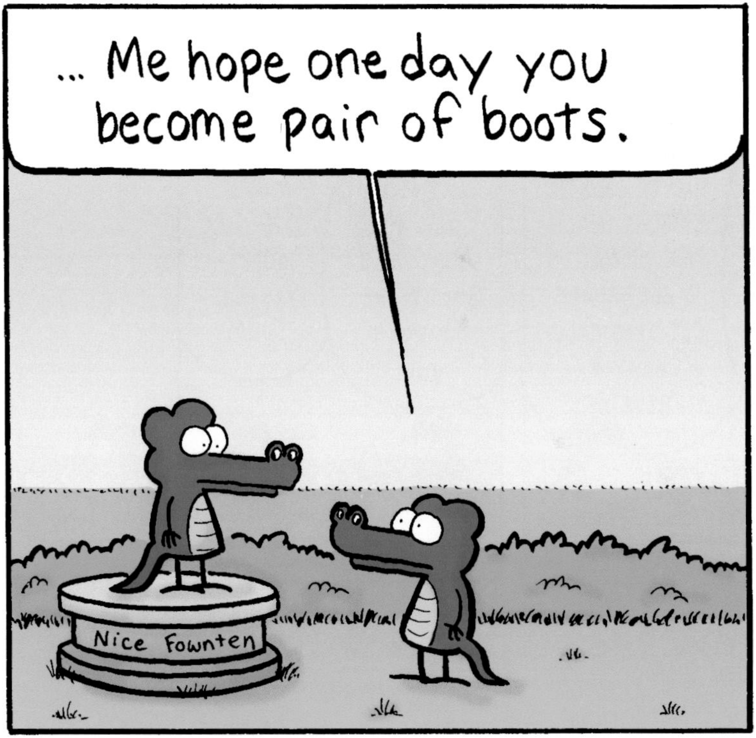
... Me hope one day you become pair of boots.
Nice Fownten

Sumtimes when you is have stoopid frend,
is better to have pare of boot

Hullo, zeeba neighba. Leesten... What you got on chest?
THEY'RE COLORED RIBBONS. EACH ONE SYMBOLIZES A ZEBRA LIFE CUT TRAGICALLY SHORT BY PREDATORS.
Dat too bad. Me wear one. Show me support you.
YOU'RE THE GUY WHO KILLED THEM.

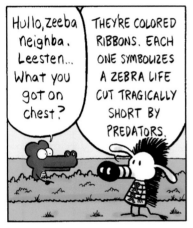

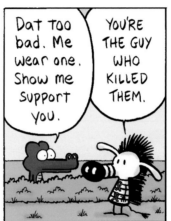

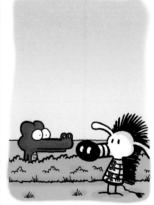

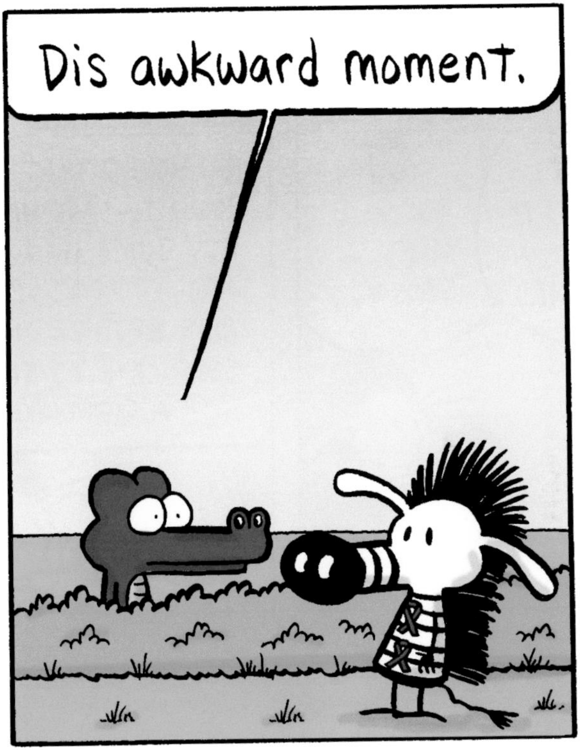
Dis awkward moment.

Crocs is have gud heart, unlike zeebas
who shood all die

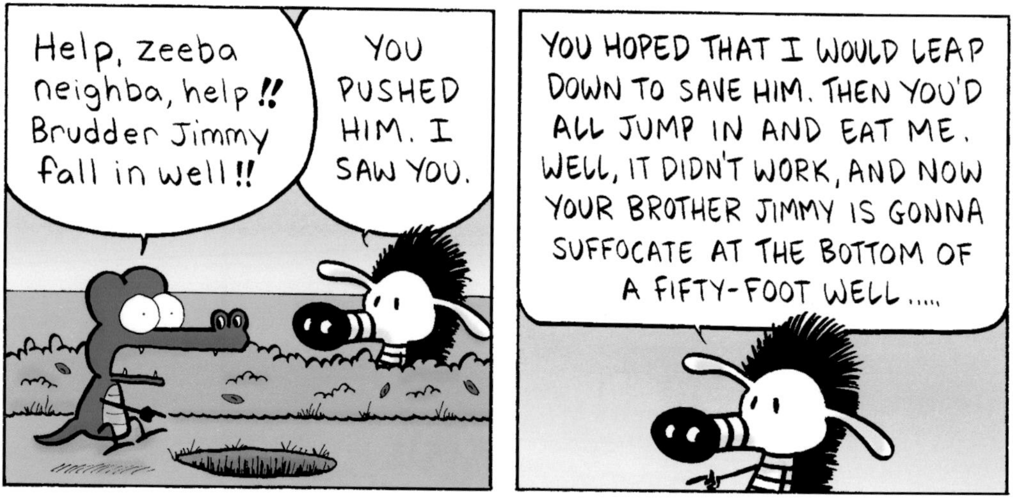
Help, zeeba neighba, help!! Brudder Jimmy fall in well!!
YOU PUSHED HIM. I SAW YOU.
YOU HOPED THAT I WOULD LEAP DOWN TO SAVE HIM. THEN YOU'D ALL JUMP IN AND EAT ME. WELL, IT DIDN'T WORK, AND NOW YOUR BROTHER JIMMY IS GONNA SUFFOCATE AT THE BOTTOM OF A FIFTY-FOOT WELL.....

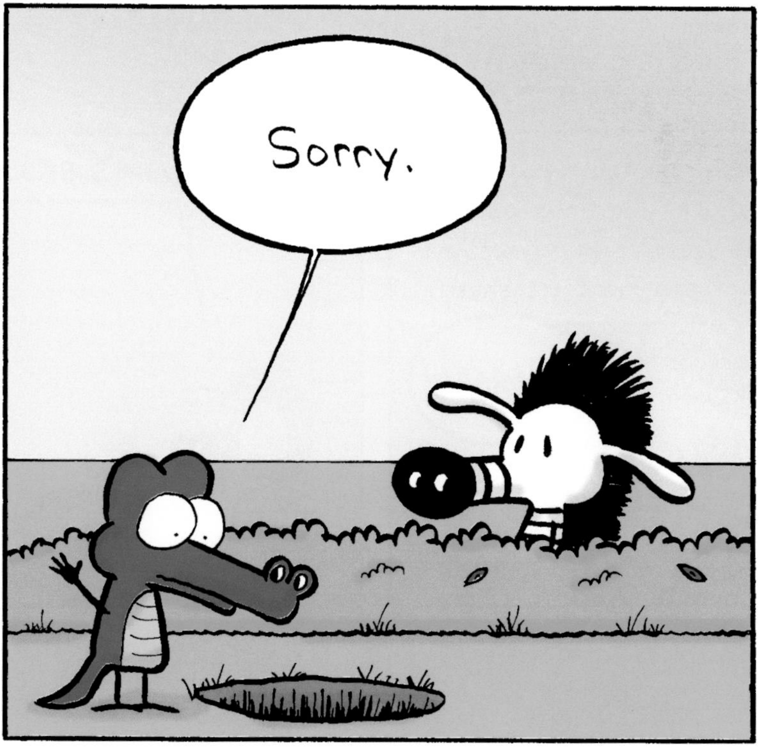
Sorry.

Frends appologise for da leetle tings

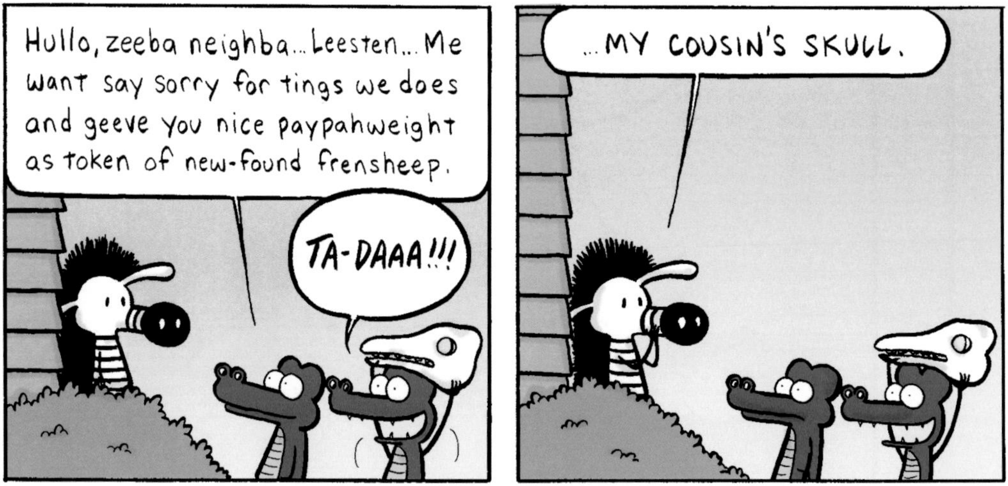
Hullo, zeeba neighba... Leesten... Me want say sorry for tings we does and geeve you nice paypahweight as token of new-found frensheep.
TA-DAAA!!!
...MY COUSIN'S SKULL.

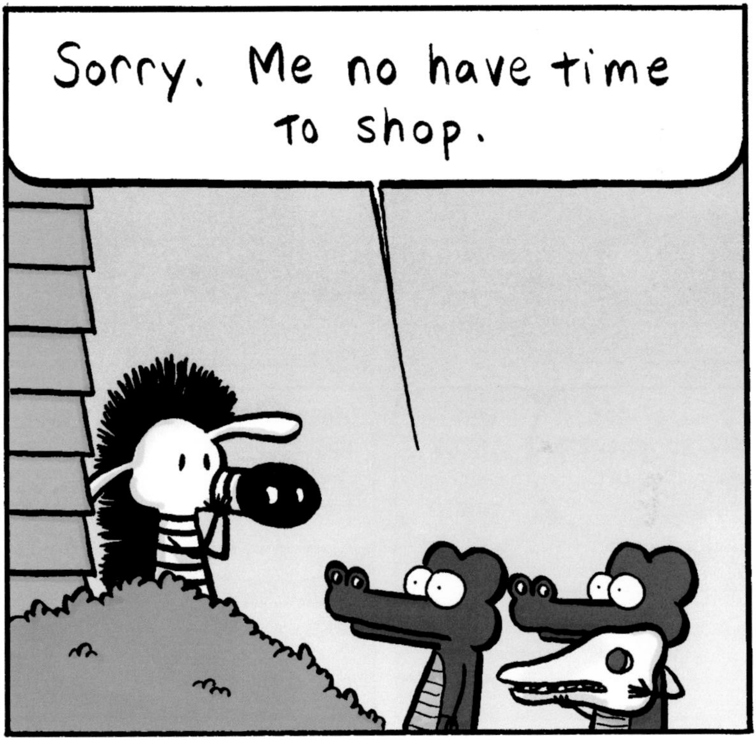
Sorry. Me no have time to shop.

Frends geev thotful geefts.

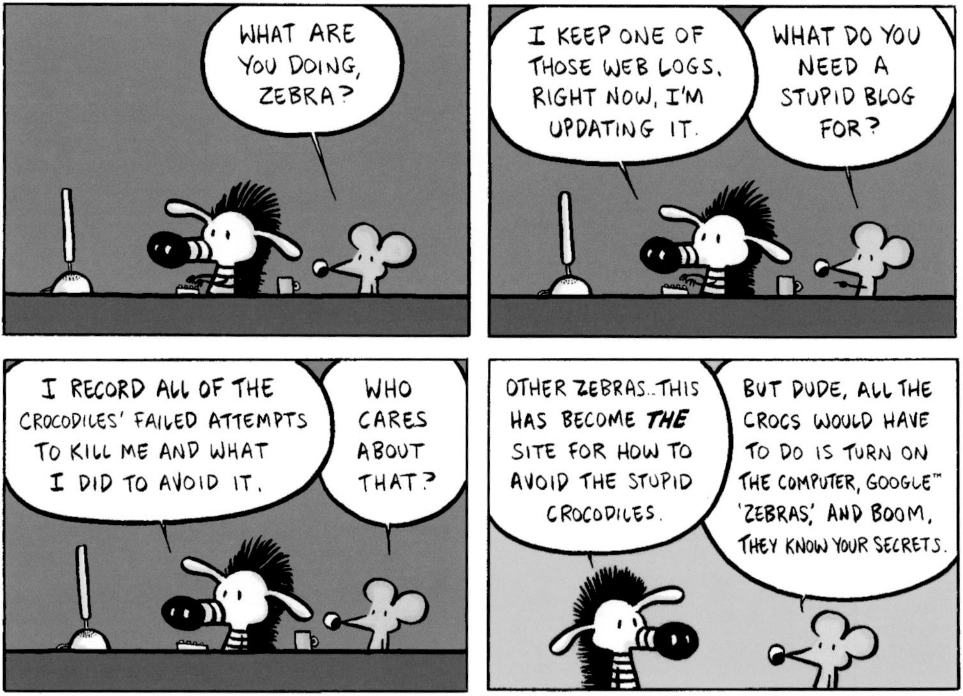
WHAT ARE YOU DOING, ZEBRA?
I KEEP ONE OF THOSE WEB LOGS. RIGHT NOW, I'M UPDATING IT.
WHAT DO YOU NEED A STUPID BLOG FOR?
I RECORD ALL OF THE CROCODILES' FAILED ATTEMPTS TO KILL ME AND WHAT I DID TO AVOID IT.
WHO CARES ABOUT THAT?
OTHER ZEBRAS...THIS HAS BECOME ***THE*** SITE FOR HOW TO AVOID THE STUPID CROCODILES.
BUT DUDE, ALL THE CROCS WOULD HAVE TO DO IS TURN ON THE COMPUTER, GOOGLE™ 'ZEBRAS,' AND BOOM, THEY KNOW YOUR SECRETS.

I'M NOT WORRIED.
Work. **NOW**. Or me keek you een hed.
Stand back, Bob. Me gonna yank his tail.

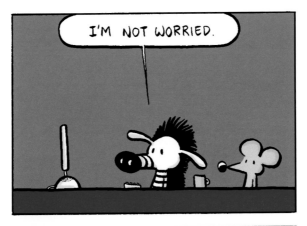

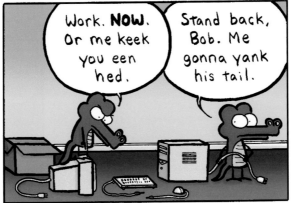

Frends help you scare applyances

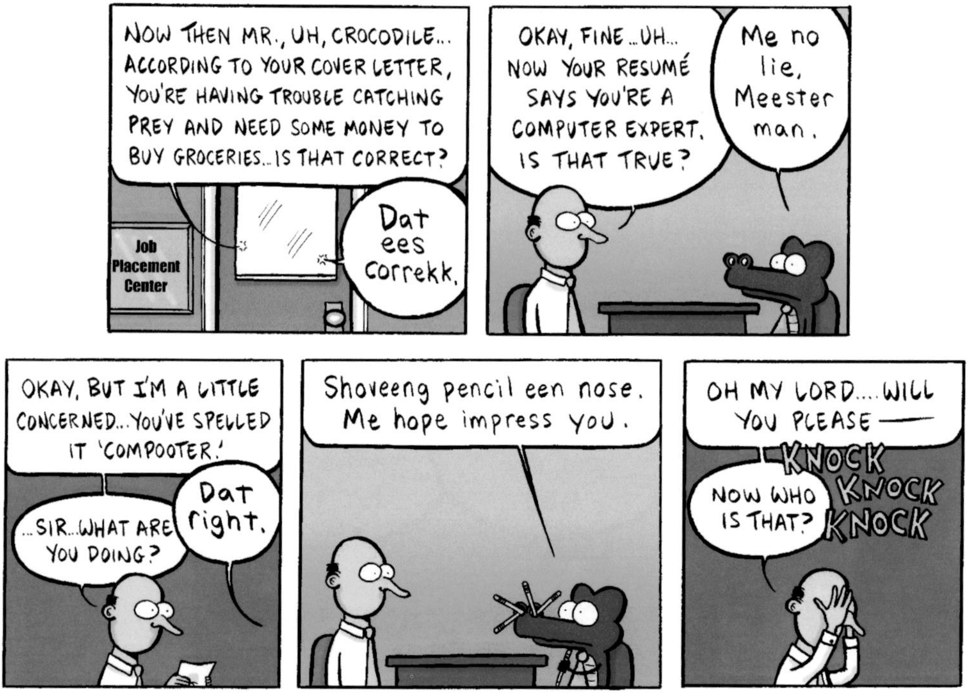
NOW THEN MR., UH, CROCODILE... ACCORDING TO YOUR COVER LETTER, YOU'RE HAVING TROUBLE CATCHING PREY AND NEED SOME MONEY TO BUY GROCERIES... IS THAT CORRECT?
Job Placement Center
Dat ees correkk.
OKAY, FINE... UH... NOW YOUR RESUMÉ SAYS YOU'RE A COMPUTER EXPERT. IS THAT TRUE?
Me no lie, Meester man.
OKAY, BUT I'M A LITTLE CONCERNED... YOU'VE SPELLED IT 'COMPOOTER.'
Dat right.
...SIR... WHAT ARE YOU DOING?
Shoveeng pencil een nose. Me hope impress you.
OH MY LORD.... WILL YOU PLEASE —
KNOCK KNOCK KNOCK
NOW WHO IS THAT?

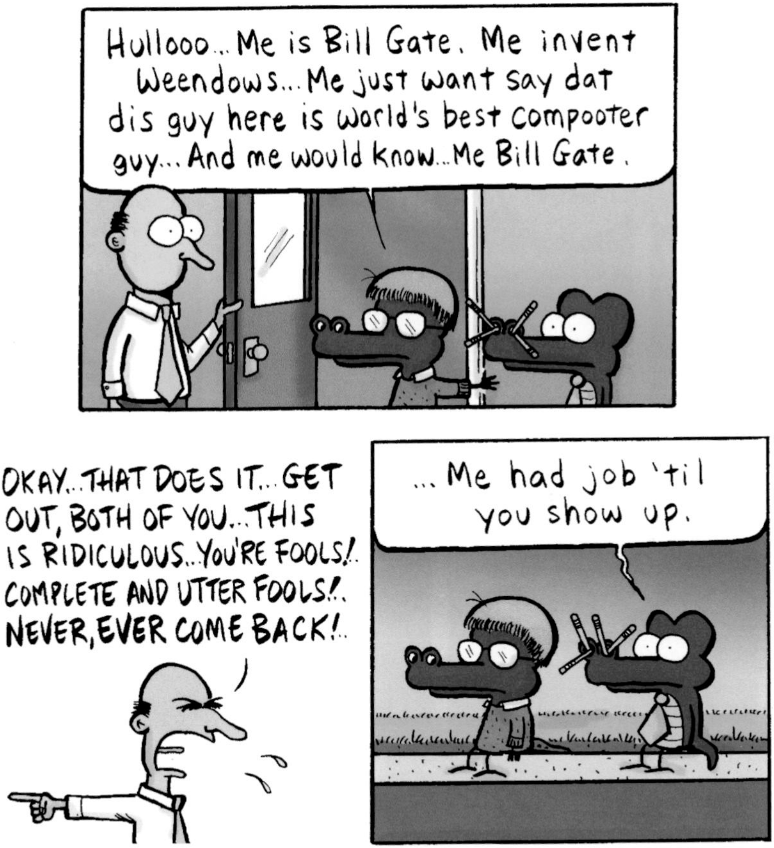
Hullooo... Me is Bill Gate. Me invent Weendows... Me just want say dat dis guy here is world's best compooter guy... And me would know... Me Bill Gate.
OKAY... THAT DOES IT... GET OUT, BOTH OF YOU... THIS IS RIDICULOUS... YOU'RE FOOLS!! COMPLETE AND UTTER FOOLS!! NEVER, EVER COME BACK!!
... Me had job 'til you show up.

(Dis commint not reely have to do wid "frendsheep" but me juss want say dis guy not reely Bill Gate)

Bob! Bob! Look at dis!
What ees it Floyd?
Ees pre-killed aneemal! Ees third one me find here dis week!
What does dis mean, Floyd?!
It mean God love us, Bob!
He do?
Of course he do! He know we have trubble catch food, so he give us some alreddy ded!
God muss have beeeg plan foh us, Floyd!! God muss have beeg plan!!

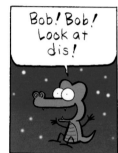

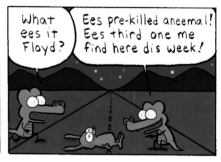

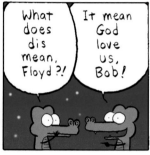

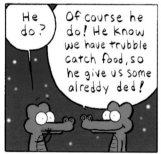

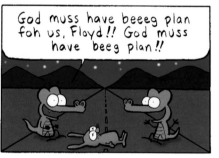

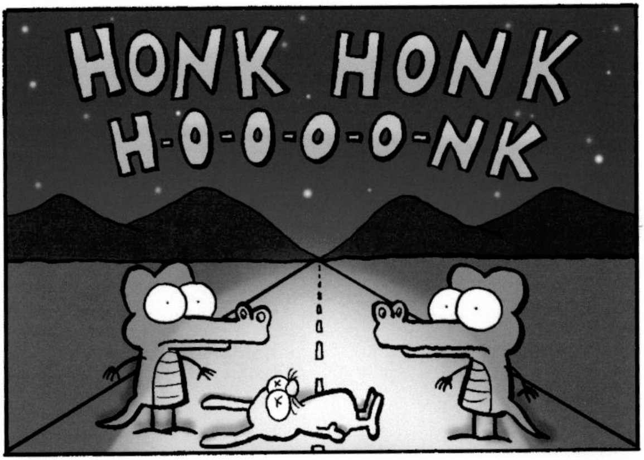
HONK HONK
H-O-O-O-O-NK

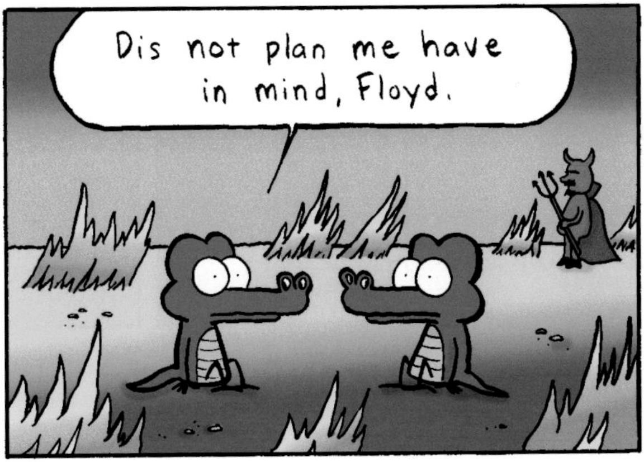
Dis not plan me have in mind, Floyd.

Frends no geet killed by trucks

WHAT ARE YOU DOING?
We practice death rolls. Crocs does it when dey catch prey in jaws. Snaps neck. Loser dies.
THAT'S HIDEOUS.
HAHA...Dat nature, pal. Show heem, Clarence... Show heem how losers die.
CLOMP
ROLL ROLL ROLL
ROLL ROLL ROLL ROLL ROLL
HONK HONK
SCREEEEEEECH
AAAAAAHHH
THUMP THUMP

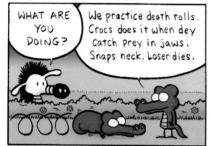

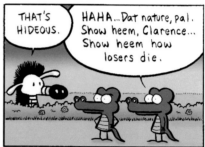

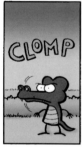

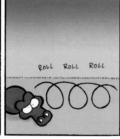

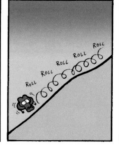

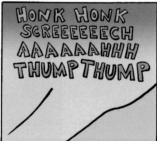

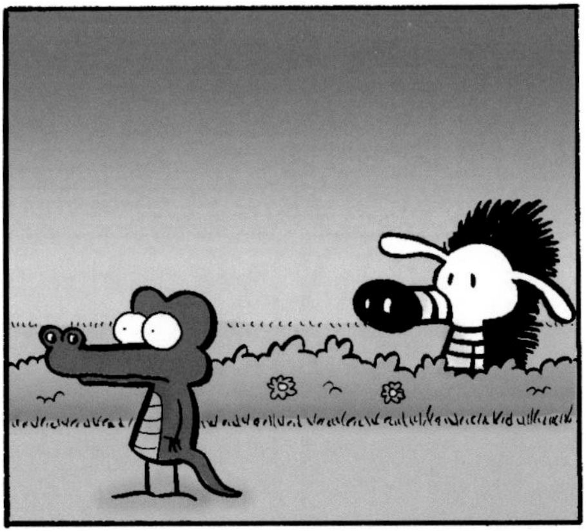

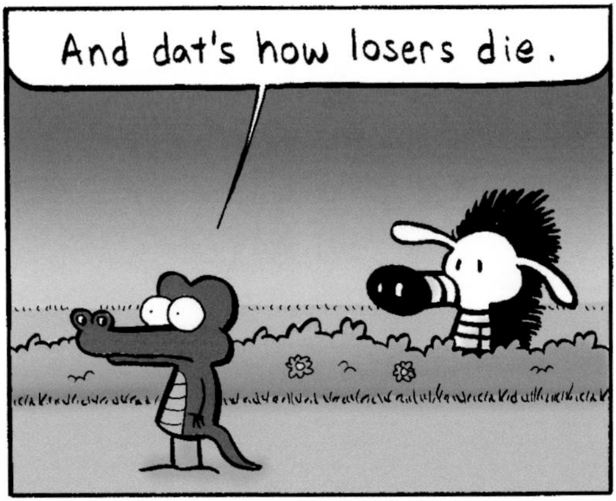
And dat's how losers die.

[Memmo to Andruw Ronald Meecdonald Publeesher of dis book: Peese stop filling book wid strip like dis one and last one. Is no repreesentative of crocs and is no appreeshiated]

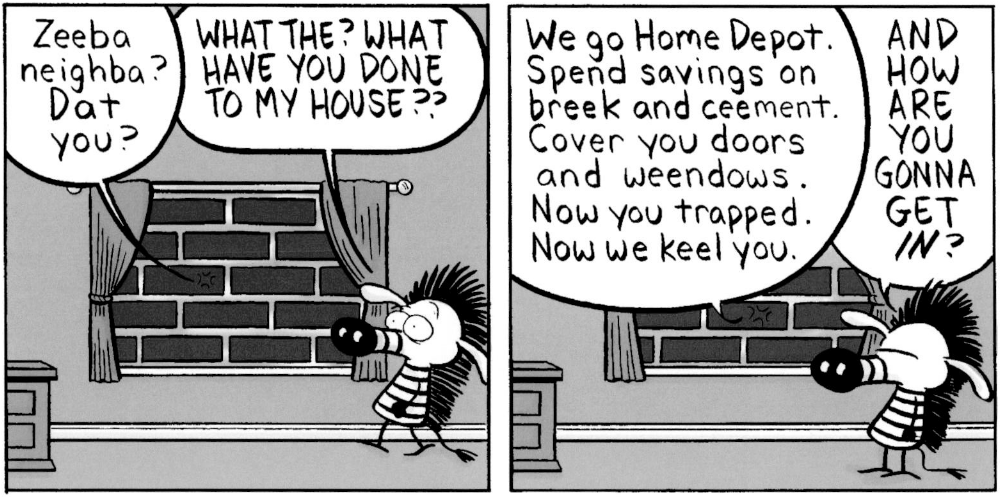
Zeeba neighba? Dat you?
WHAT THE? WHAT HAVE YOU DONE TO MY HOUSE??
We go Home Depot. Spend savings on breek and ceement. Cover you doors and weendows. Now you trapped. Now we keel you.
AND HOW ARE YOU GONNA GET *IN*?

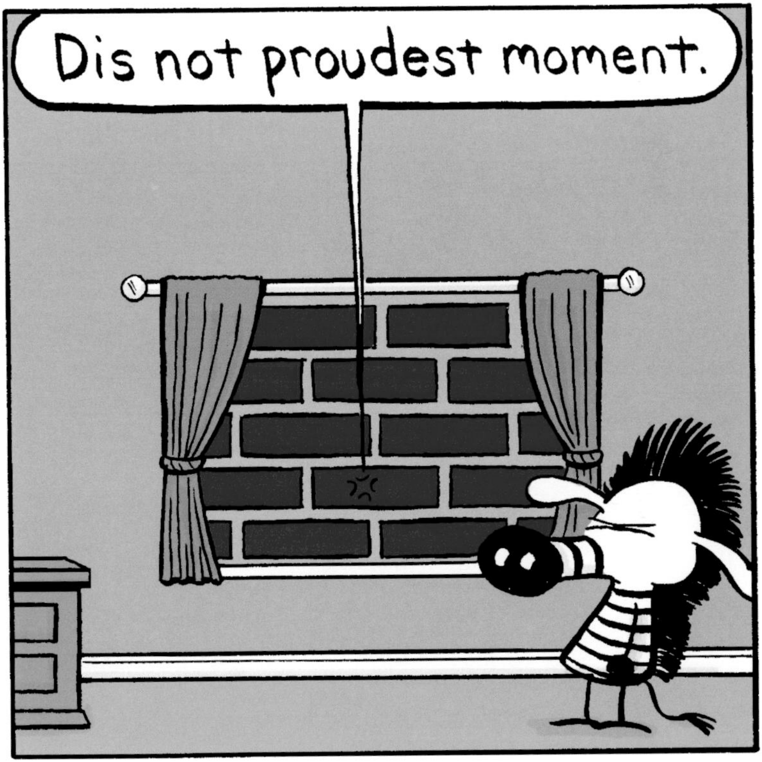
Dis not proudest moment.

[Dat THREE IN ROW.]

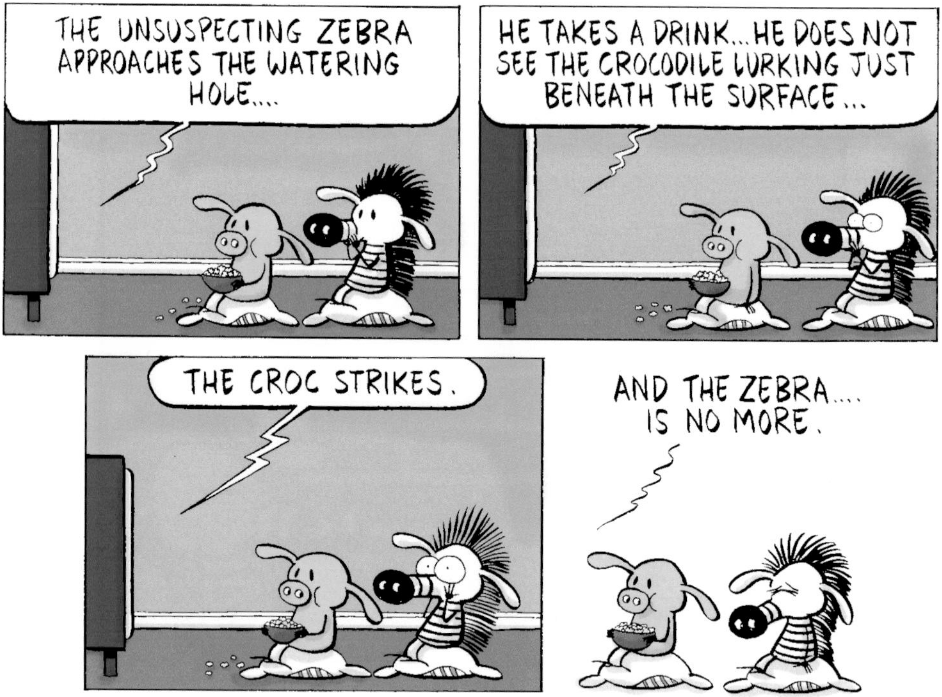
THE UNSUSPECTING ZEBRA APPROACHES THE WATERING HOLE....
HE TAKES A DRINK... HE DOES NOT SEE THE CROCODILE LURKING JUST BENEATH THE SURFACE...
THE CROC STRIKES.
AND THE ZEBRA.... IS NO MORE.

WOOHOOHOOOOOOO!
SO WHEN DO YOU GET YOUR DRAPES BACK FROM THE DRY CLEANERS?
We numba one! We numba one!
NOT SOON ENOUGH.

HAHAHAA. Now DIS gud stuff. Way to GO
Andruw Ronald Meecdonald Publeesher

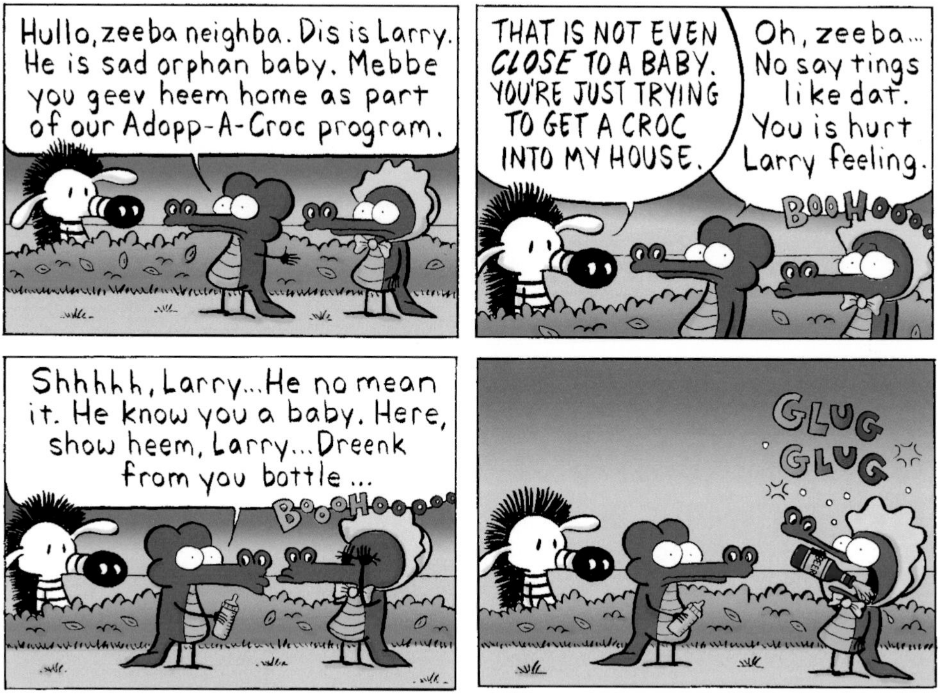
Hullo, zeeba neighba. Dis is Larry. He is sad orphan baby. Mebbe you geev heem home as part of our Adopp-A-Croc program.
THAT IS NOT EVEN *CLOSE* TO A BABY. YOU'RE JUST TRYING TO GET A CROC INTO MY HOUSE.
Oh, zeeba... No say tings like dat. You is hurt Larry feeling.
BOOHOOOOO
Shhhhh, Larry...He no mean it. He know you a baby. Here, show heem, Larry...Dreenk from you bottle...
BOOOHOOOOOO
GLUG
GLUG

UUUUURRP
BEER
Dat not right bottle, Larry.
But dis one take me to happy place, Bob.
BEER

Beer is gud. Is better den frends

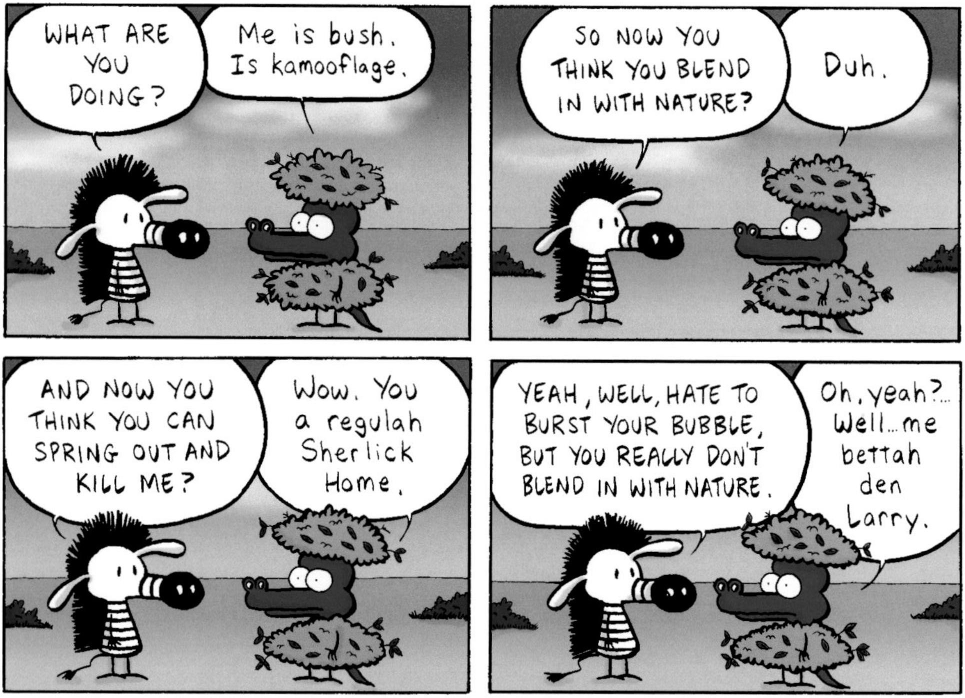
WHAT ARE YOU DOING?
Me is bush. Is kamooflage.
SO NOW YOU THINK YOU BLEND IN WITH NATURE?
Duh.
AND NOW YOU THINK YOU CAN SPRING OUT AND KILL ME?
Wow. You a regulah Sherlick Home.
YEAH, WELL, HATE TO BURST YOUR BUBBLE, BUT YOU REALLY DON'T BLEND IN WITH NATURE.
Oh, yeah?... Well... me bettah den Larry.

Frends no say to zeeba, "Wow Look My frend who wants keel you is deesguised as drying macheen"

Dear Werld Wyldlife Funnd, We hear you does gud stuff sayving aneemals like zeebas. Gud for you.
But me and Bob have better plan.
KEEL DEM
We not care how. Sticks. Stones. Brake dere bones. Just keel dem all and ship to us.
BEER
Mebbe you ask why. Me tell you. Becuss zeebas is like unnecesary horses. You no can ride dem and dey dress funny.
You know, Larry... Some people say you no can keel zeebas like dat becuss you disrupt vital link in food chain.
Hmm. Gud point, Bob. How 'bout you breeng me stamp while me correct letter?
You got it.

BEER
BEER
P.S. Peese keel Bob too.
BEER

Frends wait til frends leeve room
to say bad tings about dem

Okay, zeeba neighba.. Prepare to die. We have Mexican wrestler on our side.
HAHA Yeah.. Me crush you.
MEXICAN WRESTLERS SPEAK SPANISH.
Burrito. Burrito. Burrito.

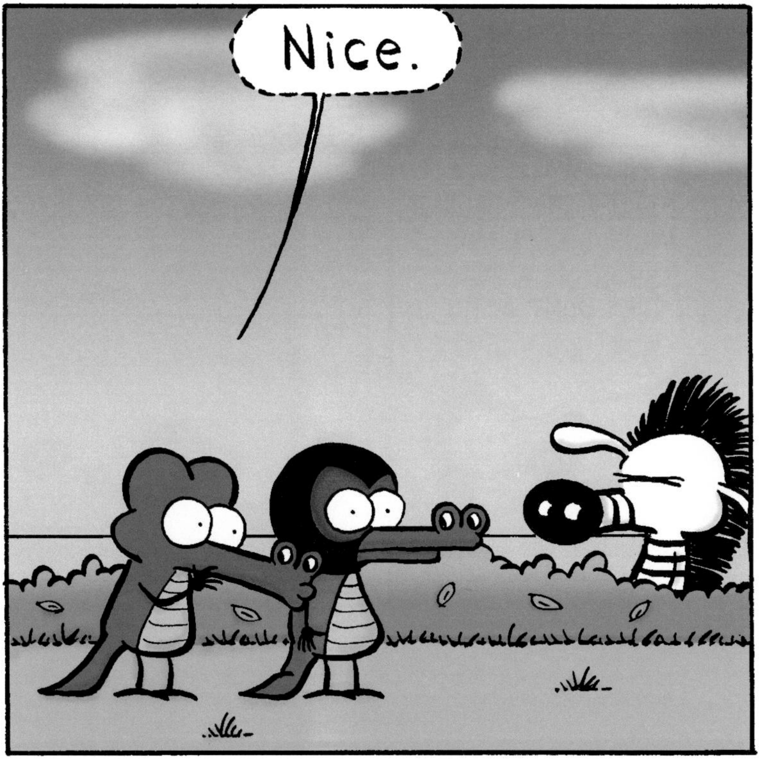
Nice.

Frends is multilinguidable

Hola, Señor Zeebo... Me is dangerouso. Me can snappo necko. You geev uppo.
Ack
YOU KNOW, THAT WRESTLING IS AN ACT, LIKE A MAGIC SHOW OR A PLAY... THEY DON'T ACTUALLY HURT EACH OTHER.
SNAP

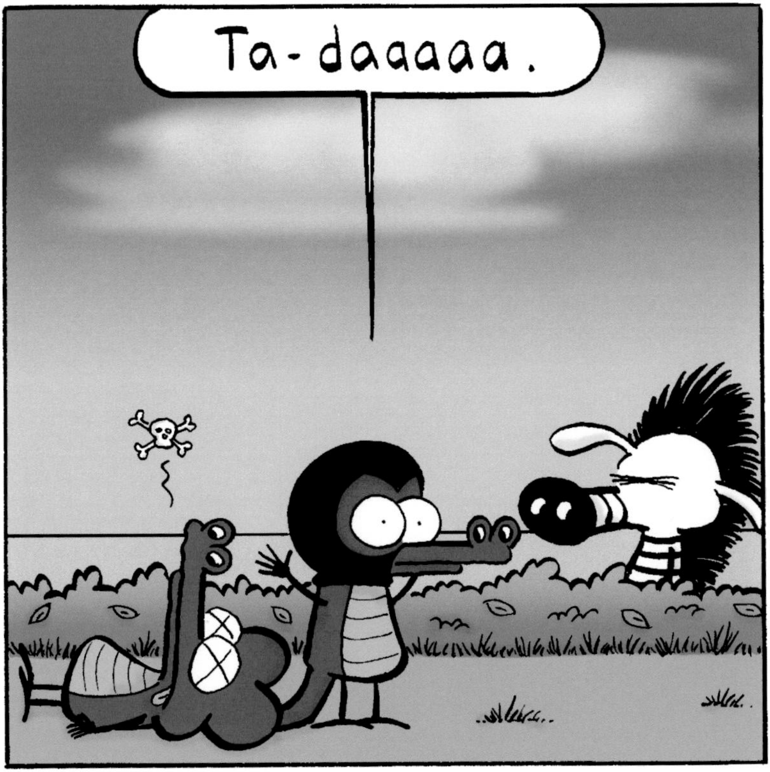
Ta-daaaaa.

[Edeetor: Peese no end frendsheep book on dis note.]